Our Schools:
What Happened?
How To Fix Them

Stella S. Crawford
Phillip L. Vandivier

Our Schools:
What Happened?
How To Fix Them

Copyright © 1998
Phillip L. Vandivier

Published by :
Psychological/Educational Publications
Post Office Box 50626
Indianapolis, IN 46250

ISBN: 1-57502-693-7

Library of Congress Catalog Card Number: 97-95307

Printed in the USA by Morris Publishing • Kearney, Nebraska

Dedication

This book is dedicated to
Vera Hilberry
Margaret Benson Enmier
Judith McBride
Patricia Friedly
Constantina Hart
Robert Hensley
Bernie Morris
and all good teachers everywhere.

Table of Contents

Table of Contents
[Continued]

PROLOGUE

Our public schools, once America's pride as a sign of our world-class democracy and achievement, have fallen out of the public's favor due to a wide variety of perceived and actual problems.

While there are no simple solutions to all the troubles plaguing our schools, our intent is to provide a number of useful, low-cost suggestions which could actually be implemented throughout the United States to help our youth become successful, happy, competent adults.

There was a time when most people associated major problems in the schools with only the very largest cities in the United States. However, as numerous examples presented in this book demonstrate, such problems are rapidly spreading everywhere. If this trend continues unabated, the very fiber which holds this country together will be destroyed.

Although identities of students are altered, all of the anecdotes in this book are true. These stories are not extraordinary but are typical of daily life in school settings in the wheat and corn belts throughout the heartland of middle America.

INTRODUCTION

Is there any doubt that our public schools are in serious trouble? Are our children learning as much and achieving as highly as they were a decade or more ago? Are our children happier, safer, kinder, more respectful, more productive human beings then previous generations?

The majority of Americans would answer these questions with a resounding *"NO,"* indicating something has gone badly amiss with our public education system.

So what is wrong with our schools? There is a tendency to look for one cause or one problem that can be solved so that everything will be fine again. However, these problems didn't develop because of any one decision or single cause, but resulted from a number of subtle influences which have been chipping away at our schools for the last thirty years--bit by bit, piece by piece, brick by brick.

As a result of many changes, most of which were made with the best of intentions, our public schools now are tottering on the verge of collapse.

This book shows the forces which have brought us to the point where we are now, and, more importantly, gives possible solutions that would restore our schools, brick by brick, to their former world-class status.

MORALS AND VALUES

People cannot live together without shared central beliefs and shared expectations of appropriate behavior. This is true for just two people trying to live together in a home or two hundred fifty million people trying to live together in harmony in a peaceful country. There will be misunderstandings, arguments, fights, wars, and finally, chaos if people living side by side don't have a shared understanding of basic beliefs and common expectations of interpersonal behaviors.

* * * * *

The leader of a taxpayer-funded workshop explained to a group of teachers the incorrectness of expecting all children to obey a common rule against stealing--the taking of another person's possession(s). The workshop presenter spoke of an unnamed village located on another continent where all the people shared and shared alike. There was no ownership, and without the negative concept of ownership, there could be no theft.

The example given was of a village bowl. One man made the bowl and used it for his immediate need. When he was finished, he sat the

3

bowl down. Another man needed a bowl to mix a porridge of local grain and took the bowl to use. Each person who needed a bowl used it, then left it for the next person to use.

The presenter did not address what happens when several people choose to use the property at the same time, or how it was decided who got to use the bowl, or what happened if someone broke the bowl.

* * * * *

The point of this story was that traditional teachers and traditional schools need to rethink their expectation that school children be taught to recognize private ownership of property. The presenter was concerned that too many young men in this country are being arrested and their lives damaged because we hold this common belief in individually-owned property.

Why would anyone care if someone "borrowed" his car while it was setting in a parking lot all day? After all, it wasn't being used by the "owner" at the time.

Many Americans now adhere to the theory that all values are flexible and that there is no intrinsic right or wrong in any behavior. While this

4

concept may be intellectually stimulating as a discussion topic, especially for young people sitting around in dorm rooms eating pizza, it is not a theory which can be put into practice without chaos resulting.

If each person decided for himself how to behave in each situation as it arose based on flexible values, we would all be so tense and nervous that we would want to live hidden from each other, like little scared rabbits.

If there is any doubt as to necessity of shared values and behavioral expectations between all individuals in our society, we need only consider the outcomes of ordinary, everyday interactions without them.

* * * * *

Jonathan put a dollar into a two-thousand dollar pop machine and got neither his beverage nor his money returned; so he began to kick, shake, and pound the machine, cracking the plastic front. When I went up to him to ask him to stop, he explained his justification for kicking the two-thousand dollar machine as a way of getting some sort of satisfaction from having lost a dollar. He had difficulty understanding why the expensive machine which belonged to some unknown person should not be damaged because of his lost dollar.

Jonathan lacked the shared belief that much more expensive property is protected from retaliation due to much less loss. He felt that one loss was equal to another, even though the monetary values were very different.

* * * * *

Donald was in front of Rayfield in the school cafeteria line. Donald stepped backwards onto Rayfield's foot and said, "My fault, man" (a typical teenage apology). Rayfield began to hit Donald, got him on the floor, and repeatedly smashed his head on the concrete cafeteria floor until Donald was unconscious. Donald was hospitalized and Rayfield was arrested.

In a meeting I had with Rayfield's mother and lawyer, it was explained to me that Rayfield's actions were justified because the other boy had hurt Rayfield first by stepping on his foot. Therefore, one physical harm, the foot-stepping, equals one physical harm, a serious head injury, with no regard for the inequality of the two situations.

This meeting came to no satisfactory conclusion as the mother angrily stormed out of the office saying, "I just hope you get raped!"

* * * * *

Should someone take what they need, even if it belongs to someone else? How should someone respond to a perceived verbal insult? Turn the other cheek and be thought weak, or strike back and escalate the assault? Why wait quietly in line if you're strong enough to push weaker persons aside and take their place? (People in some cultures do not stand in line.)

While these questions may seem to be small issues, expectations of basic manners and behavior make it possible for us to get along together day by day. We count on cars to stop at traffic lights; we expect people to pay taxes; we expect people to wait their turn. When such expectations are unmet, society doesn't function anymore.

The fundamental question about values and behavior for any community is not what is best for the individual at any single moment in time, but is instead what would life in this society be like if everyone made the decision to act like this? Societies crumble when each person acts only for his own immediate gratification, and yet many current

7

forces in our society and our schools are calling for this very thing.

Right now in our homes and schools we are not inculcating a common belief system; shared expectations which make life predictable and safe are no longer consistently being taught throughout our culture. We no longer encourage our youth to develop a personal philosophy, religious or secular, to guide them through life.

Some of this loss of commonality began to happen when court cases took religion out of the public schools. The decisions which led to this change are understandable; we are a nation which allows people to practice a variety of religions or no religion at all.

We took the Ten Commandments off the school walls and prayers out of morning exercises. Such changes were understandable because tax money that pays for public schools comes from all the people, and so cannot be spent on advocating one particular religious ideal, whether Judeo-Christian or otherwise.

However, when we took religion out of our schools, we took out our common core belief system, and we didn't replace it with anything else. Some people suggested that we leave the teaching of beliefs and behaviors to the homes, but many parents did not do it. More importantly, if each home developed its own private rules of behavior without a shared knowledge of expected behaviors from others, when these children grow up and are turned out into the larger society--without common beliefs and not knowing what to expect from others--they would face tense, chaotic, uncooperative, and unfulfilling relationships at best; and violence, fear, and turmoil at the worst.

For a while value clarification was advocated as a substitute system for core beliefs and morals. Value clarification emphasizes individual decisions of right and wrong and situational ethics. Children were presented with little open-ended plays or short scenarios. After reading these, or having them read to them, they stated their own solutions to the issues involved based on their current individual values.

This approach showed a misunderstanding of children's true developmental needs. Children do not have enough life experience to decide large issues of right from wrong. Children's minds are too immature to see the "big picture" of what is best in the long run for most people. Most importantly, these types of value activities under numerous names and programs do not recognize that children need guidance to grow into good, loving, caring citizens.

9

So our schools are in a quandary--no religious values are allowed and the secular replacements are not working, as shown by the current disrespect and disregard running rampant in the schools.

Freedom of religion does not mean freedom from morality, shared beliefs, and shared values in a culture. People crave a feeling of cohesiveness, belonging, and control that comes from expecting others to behave according to known rules. In fact, many authorities are claiming that the development of gang membership among our youth is the outcome of these unmet needs.

Teachers need society's help in guiding our youth toward moral, competent citizenship. It is obvious that teachers cannot satisfactorily lead children if they don't know what direction they are expected to take. Teachers must know what the community accepts as normal or good behavior and which behaviors the community will not tolerate.

Teachers need to get these guidelines directly from the community they serve. This community is made up of the taxpaying individuals and businesses which pay the teachers' salaries and support the schools, as well as the parents.

The mayor of the city, as well as the school superintendent and perhaps the local media, could arrange for a series of "meetings of the minds" with the citizens of the community. These meetings would be for all people who have an interest in a stable, well-ordered community, and would not be limited to parents of school-aged children. Business leaders, educators, members of the clergy of all religions, and anyone with a stake in the community could attend. The discussion topics would be morals, values, and behavioral expectations, and would address the following questions:

What does it take to be a good citizen in this community, where we live, work, and play?

What do we expect our teachers to do to help children become good citizens of this town?

What should be the consequences for those who disrupt the process for others?

This will not be an easy task. There will be harsh disagreements between some of the people involved. Such lack of agreement regarding expectations shows what a difficult job each and every school teacher is expected to perform in addition to the academic teaching which must be done.

11

No matter how diverse the community population, certain fundamental principles should emerge from these meetings. Even though many of the people may be of different religious, secular, racial, or social-economic backgrounds, they should find that they have a similar understanding of what it takes to be a good human being and to be able to live together in a safe society.

If the adult population cannot do this, and they find that their differences are so strong and so diverse that they cannot agree on the basic fundamentals of good citizenship, then the problem of that community is not just a problem with the schools; the focus then must change to what is wrong with a community which cannot come together in agreeing with general basic guidelines to life.

Furthermore, a community with this problem should not blame the schools for being unable to do what they are unable to do.

SELF-ESTEEM

A tremendous emphasis has been placed on developing personal self-esteem in the schools.

Lack of self-esteem is being blamed for all sorts of problems in the schools and in the community in general. Low self-esteem is the supposed cause of criminal behavior, depression, eating disorders, antisocial behaviors, relationship problems, learning problems, divorce, low achievement, and encopresis (defecating in inappropriate places).

Naturally, if all of these ills were due to this single cause, the schools would be justified in emphasizing the building of self-esteem. In fact, schools have been emphasizing self-esteem bolstering for some time now.

A great deal of time that used to be spent on academic skills now is used for positive esteem growth. Students do worksheets, plays, interactive activities, view movies and film strips, and problem solve in ways which are supposed to improve their self-esteem. However, despite all the time and money spent, none of these seem to be making the original problems thought to be due to low self-esteem any better. This is because self-esteem in and of itself does not promote the development of good, caring, productive human beings.

Self-esteem is holding your own self in value simply because you exist. It indicates that you have value because you are a human being, a creation of God or nature, a living person who is part of this complex universe.

Schools must not stop with self-esteem development; however, they must go much further and teach self-respect. Self-respect is the pride and respect that should be based on accomplishments. Achievements which develop self-respect in a child can range from using the bathroom correctly at age two, cleaning his own bedroom, learning Latin, or planting a vegetable garden that actually produces. Each time he does anything in a competent, capable way, self-respect improves. Self-respect also grows from making good, capable, moral choices of behavior and from helping others.

The difference between self-esteem and self-respect is very important. Self-esteem comes from holding yourself in value simply because you are (you exist). Self-respect comes from valuing your achievements, accomplishments, capabilities, and behaviors. A person needs both. It is possible to have high self-esteem and low self-respect, as shown by a person who does little in the way of working, learning, or accomplishing but who angrily feels that life "owes" him more than he gets. It is also possible to have low self-esteem and high self-respect, exemplified by a person who feels good about his actions and abilities but not in his core belief of his personal value in the world, as might be seen in an unwanted, neglected child who works very hard to achieve.

Dwelling on self-esteem and leaving out self-respect causes children to become selfish, uncaring, and unmotivated. A study was done of death row prisoners which found that murderers generally have very high self-esteem. They in fact hold themselves in such high esteem that they do not see others as being on the same level, which justifies their manipulating others for their own needs. Another study found that gang members also tend to have high self-esteem. Obviously self-esteem teaching alone won't cure students of behavior problems.

Along with helping a child learn self-respect and self-esteem, schools need to help students develop esteem for others and respect for others. They must see the innate right of others to exist on an equal footing with themselves as esteemed people of the world. They must also learn to respect others for their accomplishments, both great and small. Furthermore, children need to view all living creatures--and even some objects--as having some intrinsic value; thus they should treat them with care.

* * * * *

While waiting for the school bus, my grade-school students had been throwing rocks at some ducks' heads at a neighborhood pond. The "winner" of this game was the student who could kill the most ducks.

When I chastised them about harming innocent water fowl, they were surprised. Lonnie, the group leader, said that it didn't matter that they hit them with rocks because "animals don't feel anything anyway."

They had to be taught kindness and empathy for all living creatures.

* * * * *

Wendy came to me to complain about her stepfather. He was "always nagging" her to keep her shoes off the sofa and to use coasters for her damp cola glasses. She thought that since she was "more important than any stupid furniture," he should let her do as she pleased with any belongings around the house.

She needed to learn that while people are immensely more important than things, others' property should also be used with care.

* * * * *

Shauntel was sent to me because she was rocking back and forth in class, jabbing her desk repeatedly with a pencil, and would not respond to the teacher. She was obviously emotionally distraught. In my office she curled up into a ball on the floor, rocked back and forth, and cried. Tears and mucous from her nose were running heavily down her face, into her mouth, and on her clothes.

After comforting and calming her, I was able to elicit this story from her: She and five other teenagers had been in the parking lot of Brick City, a local housing project, loudly talking and playing music. An older guy (police later told me he was twenty-four) leaned out an upstairs apartment window and yelled at the group of teens to be quiet, as he was trying to sleep.

Shauntel's boyfriend shot him to death and then told the group not to mention the incident to anyone. The stress of this incident was very difficult for Shauntel.

17

I went with Shauntel and the homicide detective to locate the place where this incident had occurred. The police had earlier found a body in this location.

Shauntel's boyfriend had not learned to hold others in high esteem. He felt that his right to be loud was more important than another's right to sleep; and, as Shauntel told me, he felt that being "disrespected" (by being told to be quiet) gave him the right to retaliate with violence.

* * * * *

It is not uncommon for good parents to over-praise their children for meager accomplishment. They hang children's modest efforts of drawings and school work on their walls and refrigerators. Great shows of applause are given for their children's singing and performing at home. Much of the family's discretionary money is spent on the child's interests and whims.

Meanwhile, the adults criticize their own abilities, achievements, and bodies, and so deem themselves unworthy of the sort of purchases and activities they supply their children.

The children learn the message: What I do and want is important. Other people, as shown by my parents' example, are of much less value.

Many schools also reward students for very little effort. "Student of the Week" awards are shared equally. Prizes are given for doing routine activities. Young people begin to expect that just because they exist, they will be given multiple awards and praise. When they enter adult relationships and the work place--where mediocre performances go unapplauded and recognition comes to others, rather than themselves--they predictably become bitter and unhappy.

Our nation needs to calm down about minor incidents of perceived disrespect. High self-esteem must be tempered with respect, compassion, empathy, and responsibility. School programs need to place more emphasis on cultivating comprehensive personal attributes such as these rather than overemphasis on just self-esteem.

At best, self-esteem building activities can be a waste of time. And at worst, they can contribute to the violence in our society. Those few young people who truly have self-esteem problems would best be served by the school counselor or school psychologist where their problems and issues can be handled on a more individualized basis. Blanket instruction on self-esteem growth as the panacea of all personal shortcomings should cease.

LITIGATION

Lawyers and judges have done more than their fair share to cause much of the turmoil in schools today. We are not speaking here of the landmark decisions which expanded educational opportunities for all children regardless of race, creed, religion, or special needs.

There was a past time in the public schools when many children were not given the same opportunities as others. Children from the poor side of the tracks were not given the same rights to attend schools as wealthier children. Black children were segregated. Minorities and poor children found themselves in schools which did not have the quality or quantity of books or supplies as other schools. Children with serious special needs were told to stay home and were not given a chance at all. Children with disabilities as minor as a leg that was too short or a speech defect were put in special schools where they were segregated from everyone else. Some important court decisions remedied these situations and thus improved schools for all people.

There are, however, many lawyers who can't wait to take the schools to court. They see taxpayer-supported schools as a source of "deep pockets" from which they can enrich themselves and their clients. If they can win a case, they know that legal fees will be paid and that punitive damages will be much higher than if they were suing an individual. They take the chance of striking it rich by supporting what they consider to be "student rights" cases. This means that every teacher every day standing in front of every classroom has to have the following question constantly in the back of his mind: *Am I going to irritate a child or upset a parent so much that for some reason the parent is going to bring in an attorney?*

The fear of litigation is a serious problem for teachers. There have been enough frivolous cases to make teachers worry.

Is *Gone with the Wind* an offensive movie or a piece of history students should see? Does a student have the right to wear dozens of condoms in her hair as a personal statement regarding safe sex? May a teacher put tape on a student to remind him not to talk? May a student have an order of ribs delivered from a nearby restaurant during math class? Who decides if a student's clothes are inappropriate, the parents who purchased the skin-tight short skirt or school personnel?

These are examples of cases which have been taken to court by disgruntled parents. Every time a teacher does anything--tells a child to stop talking, makes a reading assignment, or asks a student to sit in a front row desk--he or she is aware of possible legal repercussions.

Lawyers look at the cases differently than teachers. Teachers are concerned with presenting a body of knowledge to an entire class while keeping the students safe. The lawyers, on the other hand, are dealing with situations from only one point of view: How does the action in question effect this one child (their client)? They totally discount appropriateness of the action in view of the teacher's need to maintain order and an atmosphere which is conducive to learning for an entire class of students.

* * * * *

I sat in a conference room with an attorney, a parent, a recorder, and a child advocate. We discussed Aaron, a seventeen-year-old male, whose mother felt was not placed in classes which would best prepare him for his future. She also felt that he was not being given appropriate socialization for someone of his age. Aaron was occasionally violent, given to frequent outbursts of talk, and often made inappropriate remarks to his classmates.

One day he went to the bathroom and smeared feces on two library books. When he tried to return them to the librarian she refused to accept them. Aaron began yelling and ripped the books up. Seventy-two of his fellow students had to hear, see, and smell this incident.

The attorney, speaking for the mother, asked me to place the young man in industrial technology classes which the mother had requested. I refused, as I had before, because I felt such classes were unsafe for her child; just as importantly, it was unsafe for the teacher and other students in the class, since we had already witnessed violent outbursts from her son. These classrooms would have readily available tools which could be used as weapons. I felt the safety of the entire room full of students overrode the need of a single student to learn to use tools and equipment.

The parent and lawyer did not agree with me. They also wanted the school to provide socialization opportunities for Aaron, including arranging for dates. I informed the attorney the school could not, under any circumstances, require or coerce a fifteen, sixteen, or seventeen-year-old girl to date any other student. There was a side discussion between parent and attorney; they returned with the suggestion that I or the school nurse should teach the young man to masturbate as an acceptable sexual release. This request was also declined.

The attorney felt my negative responses to these parent requests were unacceptable and that the school should provide for this student's social and vocational needs. I decided that perhaps this attorney was expecting too much from a public school. I asked him if he had met his client, and the lawyer said no. He had talked repeatedly both to the mother and the advocacy person, but he had never personally met Aaron.

I sent for Aaron and introduced him to his attorney. The attorney shook his hand while I snickered to myself because he had no idea where that hand had been. When the attorney started to talk, he got on Aaron's nerves. Aaron picked up a handful of large, heavy books and threw them at his attorney, hitting him several times in the head, knocking over his brief case and spilling his papers. I stood up, calmed Aaron, and whisked him out of the room to an aide who removed him to a "safer environment" with other students.

I turned back to the attorney and said, "This is why he is not in those vocational classes, and this is why he doesn't have a date."

The attorney simply mumbled, "I need to rethink this matter." I never heard from him again. Apparently being hit in the head changed his views on what should be demanded from the public schools.

If attorneys don't want to be subjected to being struck in the head, then surely the other students in the school should have the same right.

* * * * *

Acceptable community standards of school issues need to be determined within the school corporation district prior to expensive and time-consuming litigation.

While written guidelines can be very helpful for informing students and parents of school expectations, a large number of diverse opinions and subjective interpretations of school/child interactions still arise each year. Instead of immediately invoking a legal solution for every problem, why not develop an arbitration system which would resolve many such issues without the time and expense of legal intervention?

School personnel, parents, and students could all present their side of an issue to the community arbitration board. The mayor's office could appoint community members on a revolving schedule made up of people who represent all elements of the community--community and civic leaders, church leaders, business personnel--anyone with a stake in the outcome of the future direction taken by our schools.

Neither parents nor teachers would dominate the arbitration board membership because our schools belong to everyone in the community. A panel of five with a simple majority rule could decide issues ranging from whether wearing long flannel pajamas to class violates the dress code, to whether a suspension is appropriate for "forgetting" to take a box cutter out of an ankle strap before coming to school. (Some parents have insisted their sons have such weapons for protection at school.)

This board would not replace anyone's due process and legal right to go to court if he does not agree with the board's decision, but many, many cases could be arbitrated without litigation.

Remember, when cases are litigated, it's the taxpayers' money which often pays lawyer and legal fees for the school system, for the teacher, and for administrators. Furthermore, many times it's the taxpayers who are paying for the attorney representing the student client. Either way, the taxpayer financially loses if it has to go to court.

Litigation in the schools has clearly gotten out of hand. It is depleting precious resources which could be better spent on teaching our children.

Schools want to reflect the community's feelings and wishes. We just need to know what those wishes are. Community arbitration boards would provide this information.

IRRELEVANT SCHOOLS

Schools are always being criticized for being uninteresting and irrelevant, and that is why so many youths feel school has nothing to offer them. So they either attend mindlessly or not at all.

Schools are not fun. Schools can't compete with sex, drugs, and rock 'n roll, or even HBO, MTV, and shopping malls. If we try, we lose and therefore appear even more ridiculous to students, while sending out the wrong message that life should be always entertaining and everlastingly stimulating without internal effort.

Schools need not be relevant to be effective. This is radical enough to be repeated: Students do not need to find schools relevant to their current needs for school to be effective in developing competent future citizens. Hip schools and teachers started teaching students what they were currently interested in about thirty years ago. Now, classes on Madonna, skate boarding, weight lifting, and rap singing have replaced time spent on more traditional areas. Hobbies and short-lived trends are shown to students as having equal or superior value to classical knowledge when schools devote valuable learning time to cheer block, urban graffiti painting, and distance running classes, all of which have a major impact on grade point averages and class standing. The consistent refrain from students--*this is boring, why do I need to learn this stuff? I'll never use it*--begs the question.

We shouldn't teach just what students want to know or think they need to know now. Schools must educate students for their future and for our society's future. To do otherwise stresses to them the importance of their here-and-now thinking. We need to lift up their minds to greater thoughts, rather than play into their youthful, flawed, short-sighted viewpoints.

WHAT'S WRONG WITH OUR PUBLIC SCHOOLS?

Quite frequently we hear that private schools are capable of turning out a superior product for less money than public schools. However, public school costs cannot be accurately compared to private school costs because of extra expenses needed for the former to teach many, many children with serious learning, emotional, and behavior problems. As explained elsewhere, the superior product of private schools is largely due to tuition costs and admission policies which de-select the vast majority of these kinds of students--whom the public schools cannot and do not ignore.

The public schools also incur considerable costs for additional personnel due to the severity of the social problems of the children. These personnel spend many hours each week helping children cope with very serious personal problems and heartaches. Unfortunately, the cycle of problems which the public schools must handle never seems to end.

* * * * *

One of my students, Lisa, took a great many hours of my time, and my intern's time, until she

31

could get the help she needed. She was referred to me for chronic absenteeism and for being rude in class. I gave her some achievement tests and found roughly third grade skills in math and reading.

Lisa was a sullen, unhappy, pregnant sixteen-year-old. When she finally opened up to me, the stories she told sounded outlandish. In fact, my intern checked newspaper stories from her home town, and I telephoned various legal professionals to check facts and to get the student proper help.

Lisa told us her real father was a professional hit man, and so wasn't available to help her. This seemed to check out, as her biological father was in prison for killing a public figure.

Lisa said when she was young she had witnessed many violent fights between her parents. She had watched as her step-father shot her mother to death in the living room of their trailer as she (the mother) held Lisa's half brother on her lap.

Lisa's step-father begged her not to testify against him, telling her if he didn't have to go to jail, he, Lisa, and her half brother could all live together. Lisa loved her little brother and wanted to live with him again. (He had been placed in

*foster care in another state.)   However, she did
testify and her step-father went to prison.*

*Lisa was placed in foster care with a woman
the family had previously known.   Unfortunately,
her older son made Lisa pregnant.   Lisa said she
didn't want to have sex with him, and she yelled for
him to stay out of her room, but he did it anyway.
When I asked what the foster mother was doing to
prevent this, I was told she couldn't hear anything
over the noise of the TV from the living room.*

*The son threatened and scared Lisa by such
acts as tying her cat to the overhead fan, and
turning it on to show her "what could happen" if she
told outsiders anything "that wasn't their business."*

*Lisa had also witnessed the same young man
selling drugs within the foster home.   The young
man was eventually arrested for this, and Lisa was
finally placed in a more positive setting.*

*Lisa and her newborn son are doing well
now.   She is working as a helper in a long-term
nursing facility and says she loves caring for the
elderly in a calm, quiet environment.*

* * * * *

Ben came to see me one morning before classes had started. His mother had been murdered the year before, and the drug-related murder trial was about to begin.

That very morning Ben's uncle was found-- with his torso in a vacant lot near Ben's home and other body parts spread around in the street and alley. Ben thought this was because his uncle, who had cared for him since his mother's death, was going to testify at the trial.

I held Ben while he cried. He spent the entire day with me because he didn't want to go home.

* * * * *

Jonathan was referred to me because he was sleeping in class and not working. His teacher thought he might be using drugs.

Jonathan told me he had never used drugs and that he too was wondering what was wrong since he had no energy any more.

I got Jonathan the medical help he desperately needed, which he had not thought to seek out on his own.

*He had leukemia. He moved out of state
shortly after this.*

* * * * *

*I was working with Michael because of his
learning disability when his life took a turn for the
worse. He had lost the sight in one eye due to a fire
he was told he had started at the age of two. His
mother had had six children, but the older four had
been taken away by social services before Michael
and his older sister were born.*

*Michael's mother was a lifetime prostitute
who had been incarcerated earlier for selling drugs.*

*Michael didn't like the adult male who was
most involved in his life. The man had been living
with his mother years earlier when he got Michael's
thirteen-year-old sister pregnant. Social services
took that baby, too.*

*As soon as his sister was sixteen, this man
became her "husband," and lived openly with her.
Each evening he drove her to a truck stop, where
she prostituted for the family's money.*

*Michael told me he thought he could learn
to do something to make a living, like lay bricks or
work in a grocery store. He wanted to get married*

35

some day and have a regular family life. He did not want his future wife to have to prostitute to support him.

I had spoken with both a retired executives program and a Boy Scouts of America mentoring program to get help for Michael. The men in this program were going to work with Michael when tragedy struck again: His sister was murdered by a client. Michael told me how proud she was of a meat loaf she had prepared for him the night she was killed--it was the first she had ever made.

Michael came to school to be with me the very next morning. I comforted him and then asked who he was close to, who cared about him in life, so I could call this person. (His mother was reportedly very ill at this time.) He named the clerk who worked at the children's home, where he was placed while his mother was in jail, as the person he felt cared for him more than anyone else. When I phoned, I was told she no longer worked there and her new number was not available.

I went to his twenty-year-old sister's funeral. He showed me the earrings he had bought for her to wear in her coffin. It was a beautiful, touching service which emphasized not what we do to earn our living on earth, but instead, the awe and mystery of life.

His sister's friends and coworkers were there. I was momentarily surprised by their flamboyant appearance in the front rows, but immediately realized just as I was wearing my work clothes of dress and jacket, so they were wearing their work clothes, makeup, and hair. Michael was comforted by the large turnout of his sister's friends.

I met Michaels' mother at the funeral. Unfortunately, she told me that Michael would have to drop out of school; she would need him to make money to support the family now that his sister was gone.

I've seen Michael since: He seemed very pleased that I remembered him. He said he was doing okay, but I thought he was too thin and overly nervous. I asked him to come see me at work so maybe we could find a program or help for him. He didn't come. I haven't seen him since.

* * * * *

La Shawnda told me about her four-year-old sister, who had not been out of their apartment in over two years because she had no clothes which would fit her. La Shawnda reported that her mother just wasted the monthly government checks by drinking and using drugs with her boyfriend.

After I reported them, the police went to the apartment and found a naked four-year-old in the closet with significant developmental lags. The mother and her boyfriend fled. I don't know what happened to them, but I did talk with La Shawnda's grandmother, who had driven in from another city. She had been estranged from her daughter for some time, but was very concerned about her two grandchildren.

La Shawnda and her little sister moved in with the grandmother. La Shawnda seems much happier now, and it is hoped that her sister's delayed development will improve with time.

* * * * *

My secretary grimaced every time she told me that Dion's step-father was at school again to see me. I didn't much like having to spend time with him: He was loud, rude, demanding, and wouldn't follow school rules about smoking, bringing liquor into the school, or using vulgar language. He complained about teachers and staff to the point of absurdity. I thought he should get a job rather than spend so much time in his children's school.

Then Dion was hurt so badly while his stepfather was raping him that he had to be hospitalized for awhile. He began having seizures due to this trauma.

Dion returned to school but was never in very good shape after that experience. We talked together a lot, and I tried to help him get his life together.

I probably should have realized that a man who treated me so badly in a public place could be a real terror to his children at home.

* * * * *

Charlene found her uncle hanging in her garage one evening.

She came to me the next day wanting to know what it meant that he was wearing the sweatshirt she had given him for his last birthday. I surmised that he might have wanted to surround himself with good memories before he hung himself.

I gave Charlene her first cup of hot tea in my office, while telling her of the calming and relaxing effects of a fresh-brewed cup of tea.

* * * * *

I had been instrumental in putting Chad out of school for his behavior. I had even gone to court to testify against him. Yet when he got shot in the upper chest "out in the neighborhood," he chose to drive to school and come to me for help.

I held his hand while the medics worked, reminding him how tough he was, and that he would be able to make it through this, too, just as he'd always survived before.

* * * * *

Regina was pregnant again at fifteen. Her first pregnancy at age ten had resulted in a stillborn infant.

She said she started having sex at eight and a half because the older kids told her if she waited sex would be very painful. First-time sex would hurt much more, they said, after her "bones set," a process which occurred at the onset of menstruation.

Regina got pregnant again at age thirteen. This baby had a low birth weight and also died. Now she was expecting again.

I worked hard to get Regina proper care and information to help her improve her future life. Regina told her grandmother about my help. She said her grandmother had called me "an old-fashioned, good woman."

I tried to help Regina see that she, too, could be a "good woman," for herself and for her future children.

* * * * *

Cornelius told me I should check on Marcus. I found him with fresh slashes on each wrist. Marcus thought this was the only way out from the sexual abuse of his mother's boyfriend. He was too embarrassed to tell his mother what he was being forced to do after school while she was working to support the household.

His mother stood by him, and Marcus is now doing fine.

* * * * *

Courtney's mother fled the state with her boyfriend, who was reported for forcing her (Courtney) to have sex.

After the first time she was raped by her mother's drunken boyfriend, her mother put a lock on Courtney's bedroom door to keep him out. It didn't work; he was able to break the door open.

Luckily, Courtney's father was willing to take her and her brother into his home. Her father told me he had left his ex-wife when she began using drugs and drinking heavily, but he didn't think she would allow her boyfriends to hurt the children.

* * * * *

Alfonzo came shyly into my office saying he and his younger siblings had nothing to eat for dinner that evening. Their mother had been arrested the night before; her boyfriend had come by their apartment to tell them their mother wouldn't be back, and he brought them a pizza for that night's food.

In the morning, Alfonzo had gotten himself and all the other children up and on the school bus, knowing they would have breakfast and lunch and be looked after at school. But now it was Friday afternoon, with a hungry weekend looming ahead.

I asked the police why nobody had been sent to the house to help the children, and was told it is up to the arrested adult to inform them about children who needed social services help. Of course, the police would have no way of knowing about an arrestee's home responsibilities if she didn't inform them.

When informed of the young children at home, the judge said he would hear the mother's case earlier in the day, and that the charges were such that she could be released and home by 8:00 p. m. that night.

Alfonzo was happy and relieved that his mother would be home that day to take over parental responsibilities.

* * * * *

Kevin told me that he just wanted "my old mother back."

There used to be food in the refrigerator because his mother went to the grocery store once a week. All the children used to have clean clothes because Mom did laundry regularly. She used to get up in the mornings, fix breakfast, and send everybody off to school.

But now that she used crack cocaine, things were different.

43

He just wanted his old mother back--the woman he saw as his real, caring mother--not the crackhead he and his siblings now were living with.

* * * * *

These are all true accounts, as are all the anecdotes in this book, although the names have been changed.

Please do not believe these stories are the most extreme I have dealt with; actually, I have left out many more extreme examples such as fights which resulted in my physical injury and a gang member putting a contract out on me for testifying against him in court. On the contrary, these stories are all too typical of the problems facing many of our youths; they must be solved before students can study and learn effectively. While I would prefer schools which only needed to teach the three R's, the reality is that ours is a country where many of the old-time security nets are gone--neighbors watching out for children, large extended families helping each other, and church members visiting homes.

The school is one place young people feel they can turn to when trouble arises in their lives. School is a beacon which promises food, safety, and a sympathetic ear. Taxpayers are doing a great

44

service when they provide these in the schools, but the expense of doing so must be considered when comparisons of costs of education are being made. Public schools need counselors, social workers, special education teachers, and nurses, despite what they do to the cost-per-pupil expenditure.

Social problems--adult drug and alcohol abuse, physical and sexual abuse, violence, and failure of parents to be responsible, caring and good role models for their children--are harming young lives.

And this is a large part of "what's wrong with the public schools today."

DREAMS

Dreams, dreams, dreams.

If you can dream it, you can achieve it.

Follow your star.

Some day your dreams will come true.

Students are constantly bombarded with the notion of dreaming, as if young people need encouragement to daydream more hours away. This is probably one of the biggest lies that we tell students:

You can achieve your dreams, no matter what they may be, if you'll only stay true to the dream.

They need to know the truth--that even hard work and dedication will not result in far-flung goals for most people.

The vast majority of my students during the last fifteen years have expected to be doctors, lawyers, actors, media personalities, models, or

46

professional athletes, with an occasional rock star thrown in. Some shifting in goals takes place as fads come and go--nobody plans to be a break dancer any more, and rap star is fading fast. However, all of these choices are very unlikely to occur for the vast majority of my students. And can you imagine a world filled with ball players, models, and lawyers, with no clean water providers, no pizza makers, and no book publishers?

The students hear the message and they dream. Unfortunately, these dreams interfere with their real-life school achievement. Many students have told me through the years that what is taught in high school is irrelevant because their futures are set.

* * * * *

Lamont expected to play professional basketball. He scornfully told me there was no reason for him to learn math, history, or computer keyboarding because accountants and secretaries would take care of his needs when he was pulling in millions of dollars.

He refused to even try out for high school sports because he wouldn't play without pay.

He later dropped out of school. He is still waiting for his multi-million dollar contract.

47

* * * * *

Straight "F" Tasha with two children and pregnant again said she planned to be a pediatrician. Her mother pointed out in the conference about Tasha's missing classes and failing grades that this was a good choice for her daughter, since she already had experience with babies.

The mother recognized no problems with this goal for a seventeen-year-old who failed general math, reading, English, and science. They both seemed to be saying, won't wishing make it happen?

Meanwhile, they all lived on welfare.

* * * * *

We need to emphasize achievement at all levels, and we must place value on things other than prestige, money, and status. Schools have been too quick to go along with the money-status chase in our country.

Schools try to motivate using future jobs and money as the reason young people should gain knowledge. Students are asked, "Do you want to

48

flip hamburgers for minimum wage, or do you want to own a BMW? If you want the nice car, then study your science."

Students know statements like this one aren't true: Many intelligent, well-educated people are not more highly paid than less-educated people. High school dropout million dollar movie stars, fast-talking salesmen, and business owners who didn't finish college may make more money than college professors and librarians. Whores, pimps, and drug dealers' weekly incomes often surpass those of nurses, dietitians, and engineers.

* * * * *

Big Mic said, "I don't need this sh-- (referring to the educational process). I'm making all the money I need," while showing his teacher over $2,000 he was paid for holding drugs for older men. (Underage youths are often used for crime since their punishments are less severe.)

* * * * *

Sixteen-year-old Tiffany failed all of her classes because she regularly walked out of school when her beeper vibrated. Her mother furnished the beeper so she could notify Tiffany when one of her "two hundred boy friends" needed her at her mother's tanning salon.

Mom and her two daughters made a very good income with little likelihood of the girls obtaining a high school diploma.

* * * * *

Urban students laugh at us when we say an education is needed to make a good living. This statement simply isn't true. Instead, we should tell students the truth: Knowledge is to be valued because it enriches your life.

This is the message we should be sending our children. It is better to be a learned man sweeping the streets of dung, thinking of Socrates, the Messiah, and genetic restructuring than to be an ignorant man sweeping dung off the streets, thinking of nothing. True education develops an insightfulness that a man carries with him throughout his life.

While an education may never lead to riches, it can lead to enrichment, which is its own reward.

SCHOOL DISCIPLINE

Schools can do very little to discipline students. Out-of-control students take advantage of this knowledge and make school a scary place for studious youths.

Nowadays corporal punishment is nearly obsolete, the theory being that hitting children only teaches them to hit others. While I've never, ever hit, slapped, hurt, or administered corporal punishment to a student, and am opposed to physical abuse in any form, it must be noted that Japan's teachers have been known to slap students out of their seats, and a teaching friend from a well-disciplined, high-achieving school in South England tells me that she and other teachers open-handedly hit talking teenagers to the side of the head, and the headmasters use corporal punishment routinely.

I have noticed no decline of physical, acting out behaviors of students with the corresponding decline of corporal punishment in the U.S.; but I have noticed an increase in parents being hit by their children.

* * * * *

During a conference seventeen-year-old Terry disagreed with a remark made by his father. He slapped his father repeatedly until he was lying on the floor beside his over-turned chair.

The father whined in a shaky voice, "Terry, you know I wish you wouldn't do things like that," as he righted his chair.

The father never spoke again, unless spoken to by his son, and then only to agree.

* * * * *

Eighteen-year-old Shawn looked at his quivering mother while she was talking to me and said, "Shut up! You just wait until I got you home."

He routinely beat his mother and stole her money.

* * * * *

The I-can't-be-touched-no-matter-what-I-do attitude has caused some students to report their parents for abuse, even when their own behavior is outrageous.

* * * * *

Marcus came to my office to report being hit by his father the previous night. He willingly told all the details. His mother had served a dinner he didn't like.

He said, "I can't eat this sh--," and pushed his plate away. His father told him to shut up and clean up the food he spilled. Instead, Marcus stomped upstairs to his room and slammed the door, with his father close behind.

Marcus shouted, "Get the hell out of my room," and threw a lamp which broke on his father's head. His father slapped him and said he would come into any room in the house as long as he was paying the mortgage.

I questioned Marcus. He reported one open-handed slap, but I could find no marks or bruises.

Marcus was upset to learn I wouldn't have his father arrested for hitting him. He said he was never hit before and thought that all adults who hit a teenager could be sent to jail, but it never occurred to him that teenagers who batter their parents should be punished.

* * * * *

When sixteen-year-old Jennifer's mother told her she couldn't leave the house and took the car keys away, Jennifer repeatedly hit her in the head and chest with a large, heavy shoulder bag. Neighbors phoned the police.

No one pressed charges, but police did inform the parent that when a child is given a gift (such as a car) that gift becomes the child's personal property. In other words, the parent had no right to take the keys away from the child-- despite low grades, curfew violations, and disobedience.

Jennifer was very pleased to share this information with everyone she knew at school the next day.

* * * * *

Somehow many youths have gotten the message that they may not be hit, harmed, or abused without also understanding they should not hit, harm, or abuse others.

Schools cannot belittle or embarrass children. The old-time method of sitting a misbehaving child in a corner where all his peers can see his punishment is frowned upon today.

* * * * *

One parent came to me extremely agitated by a teacher's treatment of her son, Tureen. The teacher had embarrassed her fifteen-year-old child by telling him to stop his misbehavior in front of the entire class.

The mother demanded that any teacher who needed to reprimand her son should leave the classroom and take him to a private area to discuss his behavior. I was unable to agree with this request because teachers can't leave the entire class of students unattended and stop teaching that day's lesson to talk one-on-one about each momentary infraction.

Tureen and his friend were throwing one-inch long metal rods they had stolen from their industrial arts class around the room. They hit the teacher with them when she turned her back to write on the chalk board.

The mother's concern was the disrespect the teacher showed her son by saying, "This is a World Civilization Class--not kindergarten. Quit acting like you're six years old."

The disrespect shown toward the teacher and the class as a whole by Tureen and his friend

55

was less understandable to the parent than her concern that her child be protected from any embarrassment his own behavior brought upon himself.

* * * * *

Even time-out areas have been disallowed by some court cases. Removing students from class (e.g., sitting in the principal's office) has been found to deprive students of educational rights. Students cannot be required to stay after school or attend Saturday school unless transportation, child care, and parental permission issues are all addressed at the school system's expense.

Suspensions must be calculated so that all groups are equally represented. For example, you can't suspend more boys than girls (despite differing behavioral frequency patterns); racial percentages must be accounted for; special education students often receive additional rights; and number of days out and number of incidents must all be monitored in an approved fashion. All of these factors make suspending students more difficult.

Depriving students of their rights for full-lunch periods with peers, opportunities for field trips, participation in extra-curricular activities, or having students do extra duties--such as cleaning walls or picking up trays in the lunchroom--have all been questioned by the courts until school officials are afraid to do anything for fear of making a judgment error and being taken to court.

Even the teacher's right to give bad grades, retain students who don't achieve, or fail students with attendance problems are being questioned in this era of positive self-esteem and rejection of individual responsibility for actions.

Expulsion (the removal of a student from school attendance for a lengthy period of time) is decried by most of the general public as well as parents. The child is not learning while not in school. He is falling behind his peer group. He may get in trouble or pick up bad habits. Society doesn't want him on the streets where he might be bothersome or commit petty crimes.

People don't want these misbehaving youths causing trouble around town; however, when forced to be kept in school, these same youths interfere with other students' learning. Society must balance the rights of individual students with the rights of the rest of the students.

Much of this misbehavior is not simply talking out of turn, stealing others' milk money, or having food fights in the cafeteria. A good deal of the behavior schools are asked to tolerate would be criminal if done on the streets, in malls, or offices. We need to deal with this issue in our schools and deal with it seriously. It is not a matter of doing so before someone gets hurt. Everyone, including the students, parents, and taxpayers are already being hurt either physically, emotionally, educationally, or financially.

Each community must develop standards of behavior and consequences for violations of these standards. Most importantly, modest consequences should be used to mold student behavior at an early stage so that extreme penalties for severe behaviors may be avoided later. But once agreed upon, they must be consistently applied, or their effectiveness is lost.

Unfortunately, the same people who should be clamoring for our schools to be made safe havens for learning often take positions which make the attainment of this goal very difficult. Two examples which deal with weapons control will illustrate this problem.

* * * * *

Most people would think that a rule that bringing weapons to school will result in expulsion would be simple to enforce because everyone wants children to be safe from violence in school.

Several years ago one student killed another by cutting his throat in the school cafeteria. After this incident, a neighboring suburban school corporation passed a ruling that anyone bringing a gun or knife to school would be expelled for one semester.

However, when a girl was found with a knife and was expelled, several local newspaper articles were critical of this decision; many in the community argued in her defense, and some even contributed money for her legal fees.

The girl was from a "good" family and got reasonably good grades. She said she needed the knife for a class, but the teacher denied this requirement.

This was a front-page issue in the local papers until the problem was solved by her family and community donors paying for her private schooling.

What will this community do about its no-weapons rule the next time someone shows up with a box opener or a carpet cutter--two very dangerous and currently popular weapons?

*   *   *   *   *

The second example happened in a large urban school.

Raul brought a loaded gun with dozens of spare bullets to school with a plan to shoot a number of people. He was arrested and the expulsion process began.

Raul's lawyer said he couldn't be expelled because he was in a program for his emotional problems, and special education students have special due process rights. His behavior (bringing a loaded gun to school) was consistent with his being emotionally handicapped; therefore, he should be allowed to stay in his regular high school building as stipulated in his individual educational plan.

What about the rights of Raul's fellow students and teachers not to be shot at school?

*   *   *   *   *

JUVENILE JUSTICE

Juvenile crimes should be divided into two separate groups, each needing to be handled differently. Many of the disagreements in debating an effective way to stop juvenile crime stems from a lack both of dividing the two sets of problems and handling each differently.

Crimes against property and behavior standards, which we call Division B crimes, need to be dealt with very differently than severely violent crimes against people, designated Division A crimes.

Common juvenile crimes--truancy, shoplifting, theft, burglary, robbery, malicious destruction of property, assault, and battery without serious damage are all Division B crimes. Division B crimes would be completely removed from public records when the child reaches age of majority, and the child's privacy would be respected in the media. However, juveniles committing such actions would suffer consequences as soon as such behavior began.

Currently youths often "get away with" breaking laws in that they are given no punishments, and no consequences result from their illegal behaviors. They then lose respect for adults and our system of law and order, mistaking compassion and

61

tolerance for apathy and ineffectiveness. As they get by with more and more, the crimes escalate until the final punishment must be harsh due to the severity of the crimes.

We do our children no service when we allow them to get away with crime. Instead, we nurture the growth of an out-of-control society where all of our children must live in fear and unrest. Even today the majority of victims of juvenile crime and misbehavior are other children.

We must protect children from each other as we help each child grow into a kind, responsible, adult citizen.

* * * * *

A store owner phoned school because she caught a student shop-lifting beer. She wanted someone to come get him and take him back to class because she didn't want him to miss any more school or get into more trouble.

She was shocked by the advice to phone the police. She wanted to help the youth and didn't want him to get into trouble for his "escapade."

She didn't understand that allowing him to suffer no consequences for truancy, theft, and breaking under-age drinking laws would not be helping him become a mature, responsible citizen.

* * * * *

We have millions of kind-hearted adults who want to protect children from the consequences of their own actions. But in the long run protective measures are not doing young offenders any favors. Children who break the law and get away with it are likely to break the law again.

Even after an arrest has been made, our juvenile justice system tends to mishandle the problem so we get more recidivism. Young criminals are not very worried about being arrested. They know the penalties will not be too unpleasant.

* * * * *

An urban high school had to have more than a dozen youths arrested for gang fighting before 9:00 a.m. on a school day. These students were arrested, processed, and released by the authorities before noon.

All the students returned to school to resume the fight the same day. The police had to be called again.

This incident showed other youngsters that neither the school nor the police could keep away the trouble-makers for even a day, that arrests are truly revolving doors, and that juvenile justice is neither to be feared nor respected.

* * * * *

When arrested for more serious crimes and detained in juvenile justice centers, students are routinely taken to ball games where they get special treatment and autographs from the players, taken swimming and on trips, allowed to shoot pool, and to play video games. Court-issued clothing is worn like a badge of honor after they are returned to school.

* * * * *

After arresting a young man, a policeman reported back to me that on arrival the intake clerk told the boy, "Oh, good--you're just in time for the party."

She had to hurry with the paperwork so he wouldn't miss any of the pizza-party mixer for the young boy and girl criminals.

* * * * *

When youths are rewarded for inappropriate behavior, it is no surprise that we get more of the same. Many, many years of behavioral science research have established this undeniable fact, which our society continues to ignore.

A better system for these Division B infractions would be short, but very structured stays in our juvenile facilities. Twenty-four hour to eight day stays in a lock-up facility--which is viewed as a negative consequence--would do more to change some youths' behavior than longer terms which emphasize self-esteem development and personal pleasure.

Youths would be fed healthy, decent food but no tacos, pizza, hamburgers, sodas, or deserts. TV viewing hours would be limited and only G-rated classics which demonstrate positive values would be shown. No pool tables, air hockey, card games, videos, or video games would be available, but lots of good books would be available as well as simple art supplies.

Reading, math, and study skill tutoring should be supplied. No rap, hard rock, or other popular music would be played; however, a daily newspaper would always be available.

Juveniles would be permitted very little socialization between themselves and no unsupervised, unstructured time. These measures would help keep them from learning new bad habits from each other and from bragging about past and future exploits. Combination sleeping/study rooms should be small singles much like college dorm rooms. Current larger room facilities could be partitioned with wall dividers purchased fairly cheaply with the money saved from junk food and video games.

Since there would be no carry-over into adult life of these sentences, they could be viewed as growth-enhancing rather than labeling and punishing.

The current trend of parents hiring lawyers to portray a child as "not guilty," even when they know he is, is very damaging to the child. The child's mind must then grapple with the issues of his parents' lying, his own lying, the lawyer's twisting of information, and the system's apparent disregard for truth and justice.

We are not advocating the denial of equal protections for children, but parents need to be aware how damaging the exercise of this right can be to children who are clearly at fault. Most students under eighteen years of age have trouble dealing with this situation without becoming cynical and confused about our system of justice.

* * * * *

Travis was brought into my office by Officer Sanders to be checked for weapons; he had been in a fight the previous evening and was rumored to be armed and seeking revenge.

I placed the eight-inch knife the officer found in Travis' jacket on the desk and started to phone his mother. Unfortunately, when I let go of the knife, Travis grabbed it, turned, and thrust it towards Officer Sanders' chest, missing only because Sanders jerked backwards and swung out at Travis.

I yelled "No, no! Stop! Don't!"--much as if I were asking a three-year-old to stop doing something dangerous.

Sanders' immediate verbal response was "You f--king a--hole!"--a fact which was later brought out by Travis' attorney, since it was inappropriate language for school personnel to use towards a child--even if he is trying to stab you in the chest.

When Officer Sanders struck or pushed Travis, he dropped the knife and went across my desk, knocked over the computer and telephone, and then hit the wall, cracking the wall partition.

Travis then lunged at Sanders, knocking him to the floor, where they both struggled. I tried to get out to seek additional help, but the door was blocked by their rolling bodies and overturned furniture. I couldn't call anyone because my phone had been broken.

I saw Travis pull out a second knife he had strapped to his body and draw it back to stab Sanders in the back. I yelled for Sanders to watch for the new knife and asked Travis to please stop while trying to step on his hand to get him to drop the knife.

Travis cursed and threatened Sanders the whole time.

Sanders finally got his hands around Travis' neck and choked him until he dropped the knife. I removed Sanders' hand cuffs from his belt and handed them to him so he could handcuff Travis.

Even when cuffed, Travis cursed, spat, and tried to kick the officer in the genitals.

The next day Travis' mother and lawyer came to school. Pictures were taken of my cracked wall where Travis had landed. I was informed that pictures had also been taken of Travis' bruised back and arm.

The attorney suggested that Travis only had been acting in self-defense because he was afraid of the school officer; he thought a man in uniform might hurt him, and therefore tried to defend himself. I assured the attorney that I would have kept Travis safe if he would have obeyed me and calmly sat down. All parties involved were of the same ethnic background, and so race was not a factor.

Travis' mother and lawyer then said if Officer Sanders had not been in my room when Travis got upset, I would have never pushed him so hard that he cracked the wall and sustained several bruises. I agreed. Had Travis lunged at my mid-section with an eight-inch knife, I would have been stunned and would not have known what to do; thus, I would have been stabbed. And Travis' troubles would have been much greater because actually stabbing a teacher is still a serious offense.

Travis' mother said she didn't want her son to pay for this mistake in judgment. I warned her that if he got off completely without any *consequences that this type of behavior would likely continue. While her attorney felt that Travis had a chance of getting off completely, I suggested that the lawyer should ask at least for house arrest, rather than trying to prove that he was not guilty of any wrong-doing. By so doing, Travis would be more likely to learn to be more responsible for his behavior.*

This arrangement (house arrest) was made, and Travis changed schools at his parents' request. Some time later I saw him again. He was friendly toward me, reported some success at his new school, and was making money working part-time at a movie theater.

I wished him luck and happiness in his new life.

* * * * *

Perpetrators of the very serious crimes, Division A crimes, are much more difficult to deal with in a school setting. The reasons such crimes are committed may be psychological in origin, but they are harmful enough that the perpetuators must be removed from the community because of the damage they do to others.

70

Mankind has not yet discovered quick, easy cures for those who violently rape, mutilate, and kill. Sometimes maturity, counseling, or religious conversion can help these people lead relatively normal lives back in the community, but all of these take time, and the offenders can do great psychological and physical harm to other citizens if allowed to return to regular community life too soon.

Whether victim or victimizer, abused or abuser, a perpetual cycle continues dragging in new individuals who all too often are innocent children.

The treatment for these more violent students shouldn't be viewed as punishment used to modify behavior, as it is in Division B crimes, but as a simple recognition that some poor souls cannot be trusted to live among us--at least not without supervision and modifications of freedom.

* * * * *

I attended a workshop given by state attorneys on juvenile crime. Emphasis was given to the criminal's background. If he had been neglected, sexually or physically abused, or had an IQ somewhat lower than average, then it was felt he should not be held as responsible for his behavior by a compassionate justice system.

71

The problem with this practice in real life is it allows past victims freedom to behave in such a way as to create new victims--who may then victimize more and more people until everyone is a victim and nobody is responsible for their behavior.

* * * * *

Justice has a duty to protect the innocent from the guilty that is even more compelling than sympathizing with the accused.

Many young criminals can be helped with counseling to return to a regular school placement; but some who have committed violent crimes need to continue their education by mail, GED classes, or adult-only programs.

School children need to be protected from possible harm from known violent criminals. Nearly everyone would agree with this statement. But some people want young violent offenders to have a "second chance," and not be labeled "bad" by society, in fear the child will live up to that label. They hope that one or two years in a correctional facility with counseling and care has turned a child around. So do I. However, I don't want to gamble on the outcome by risking the safety of other innocent children in our public schools.

I believe that there are some consequences in life for behavior, and that one of them is that violent criminals should lose their privilege to attend regular high school, join clubs, and go to the prom. This is not so much a punishment for them as a protective measure for our other children.

I have had some success counseling young criminals back into the school setting. Many have been able to complete their education and adjusted well to school. However, I have had less success with murderers and violent rapists and strongly feel that they should not be returned to regular schools since students and parents cannot be guaranteed safety from violent behaviors. Whatever is damaged inside a youth that allows him to rape, mutilate, or murder needs more help than a school counselor with five hundred other students to look after can give. They need to be taught elsewhere.

* * * * *

Torrence was a shy, sweet, sad, quiet seventeen-year-old whom I saw three times a week for individual counseling at school. This was quite intensive for a school setting where counselors are expected to work with hundreds of children each week.

Unfortunately, Torrence was on parole for violent rape.

Torrence had been neglected all of his life by an alcoholic mother and an unknown father. His latest crime was the rape of an eight-year-old who Torrence had assured me had "wanted it," as had all the females he had molested.

Questioned as to how he knew this, Torrence said that women "crossed their legs" to tell him they wanted to have sex with him, or sent out other subtle messages. The eight-year-old had crossed and uncrossed her legs several times in his presence, which is why he raped her.

Torrence needed love, caring, and self-worth. I gave him what I could during counseling sessions and sent him out into a big school with hundreds of girls crossing their legs and flipping their hair.

It wasn't too long until he cornered a girl in a short hallway near a girls' restroom. He attacked her, pushing her into a wall, tearing her clothes, and biting her. She fought back, finally swinging a steel door into his face, and ran to my office to report the incident. I knew by her description who to have security police bring to me.

Torrence was cheerful and unconcerned about his bloody face. He said it was a mistake; he had thought the girl had wanted to have sex with him when he had spotted and watched her across the classroom. But he realized he was wrong when she bloodied his face.

Asked if her running away, fighting him, and yelling had not suggested she wasn't interested, he replied, "That's just part of the game girls play."

I phoned his parole officer and told him the temptations for Torrence were too much for him to handle, and that I couldn't be responsible for other students' safety around him.

Torrence's parole was revoked and he was returned to a correctional facility. My heart bled a little for the sweet, shy child he had been, and for the man he should have grown to be, but the safety of the innocent had to prevail.

Torrence wrote me several letters from prison. His life was so empty of caring adults that he used his free long-distance Christmas call to telephone me at my office.

He came to see me at school after his release. He was starting a construction job and seemed content.

I hope he now has his sexual urges under control, and I wish him nothing but the best and brightest future. One thing was for sure. He used his jail time to work out and develop his new buffed muscular body; nobody could fight him off now.

* * * * *

A fourteen-year-old freshman girl came to me to complain about the demanding, controlling behavior of Reggie, a new eighteen-year-old student. He yelled at her, pushed her around, demanded dates, and phoned her home continually.

Reggie said he was in love with her, and she belonged to him. She thought he was cute but a little scary. I talked with Reggie about backing off but he didn't see my point, as he knew this girl was right for him.

Reggie had returned from high school after serving two and a half years for beating his fifteen-year-old girlfriend to death with a baseball bat.

Having served his time, Reggie was not being monitored by the justice system. However, I monitored his behavior as a high school student and found that he was failing all classes, taking younger students around the city in his car during school hours, telling them tales of criminal behavior, threatening violence against students he didn't like, and stalking girls who appealed to him. I removed him from school enrollment because of these behaviors.

I wish him well and hope he has a good life but firmly believe that murderers do not belong in a regular public high school, in the interest of protecting innocent children.

* * * * *

WELFARE, SSI, WIC, ETC.

Why do you work? Why does anybody work? A lot of young people today are asking themselves this question. Many of them believe that if you work, you give up a great portion of your life doing some sort of labor for somebody else, or producing something that someone else will enjoy. They also understand that if you don't work in this country, what you get is one hundred per cent freedom and a somewhat reduced standard of living.

True, you might have to live in subsidized housing; you have to fill out forms; you have to go through some steps; but think of the rewards: You get to control every day of your life. You don't have to get up at 7:30 in the morning; you don't have to take any stuff from a boss; and you can do exactly as you wish with your time. You might even work occasionally in legitimate or illegitimate pursuits to add to what you get from various government subsidies.

Because of this present situation, many students are seeing no advantage to learning or to working. It's hard sometimes to even give them reasons why, if they can get a monthly check, can get reasonable housing, and have their food and basic needs met, they should give up forty, fifty, or more hours a week of their lives to work.

Many of our urban students have no working parent in the home at all; they have no role model of a person who gets up and goes to work regularly. Although their family might not live as nicely as we would expect for ourselves, they have cable TV (many of them have all of the cable stations); they have video games; they have $175 sports shoes; they have cellular phones, they have call waiting, call forwarding, and voice mail; they have a three-bedroom townhouse; and they don't have to do anything for all these things. Nobody in the house has to do anything for all these things. So when we tell them they've got to learn and do their school work--to prepare for their futures--their response is, quite accurately, "No, I don't."

Our well-intended "welfare safety net" which has been in place for the last thirty years has been viewed by too many young people as a sure way to get a small share of the abundant material goods available in this country. While we cannot fault youngsters for finding the quick, but short-sighted path to money appealing, we as adults should take care not to mislead our children. Easy reliance on welfare serves only to doom their future.

* * * * *

A fifteen-year-old new mother returned to my classroom with new, very expensive boots. When other students admired them, she told them they were purchased with the check she now got since she had a baby.

The other girls without babies or new boots learned of a new way to get expensive clothes.

* * * * *

A fourteen-year-old girl came to my office saying, "I think I'm pregnant. Now will they get me my own apartment?" She mistakenly thought that "they" would set her up in her own private apartment and would provide all of her living expenses. Just because she had had sex at a young age, she could live like an independent adult without working or going to school.

I explained the fallacy of her plan. Luckily, we found she wasn't pregnant yet, so she stayed in school.

* * * * *

Jackie came to school showing photos of her baby. She wanted the attention and special privileges which young mothers receive--longer lunch hours, shorter school days, special times to socialize with other young mothers--and the status which comes to them from other teens who have given birth. The photos were not of Jackie's child, but were of her cousin.

Jackie had never been pregnant, wasn't dating anyone, and was a good student.

* * * * *

Denise returned from summer vacation, all smiley and happy, telling me, "Guess what? I'm pregnant! I'll bet you didn't expect me to get pregnant this summer!" I said, "no," because Denise was a quiet, honor-roll student who had college attendance as a goal.

I asked about the baby's father; she said it was Snake--the only name she knew him by. I suggested she go ask him his real full name, because she or her child might need to know it some day.

He didn't tell her, and he left the neighborhood.

* * * * *

When visiting a home regarding child abuse toward a younger son, I met the boy's mother and teenage sister. While we all sat talking in the living room--as I made a written record of all the son's bruises and cuts--I asked how the mother got along with the daughter. She said, "Fine, now that Melissa is bringing money into the house."

The mother explained she was referring to the welfare checks for her new granddaughter.

* * * * *

Katrina's mother had five under-age daughters living with her. She received government aid for all of them. Four of the girls each had their own babies, and those babies also received government aid.

Altogether, the household income was such that ever working was not in any of their plans.

* * * * *

Rene explained to me why she and other girls don't put the father's name on the birth certificates of their babies: The fathers promise to give them money if they don't list them, and this way the government can't come after them for child support.

She said the young mother can get full welfare benefits, plus the money the men will give them each month. Therefore, she said, they will come out financially ahead.

Actually, these men have little intention of supporting their children for eighteen years.

＊ ＊ ＊ ＊ ＊

Dominique had rickets and needed painful, expensive surgery to straighten his crippled legs. Rickets should never happen to a child in this land of over-abundance.

It was apparent that his mother had used the food stamps for other things than nutritious food.

＊ ＊ ＊ ＊ ＊

I was asked by several teachers to do something about Joseph. He smelled so badly nobody wanted him around them.

Joseph explained that he washed his clothes each night in the bathroom sink using a bar of hand soap. He then hung them over the bath tub to drip dry, only the clothes didn't completely dry; so he had to wear them damp, as he had no other clothes.

The smell was from mildew and incomplete cleaning.

Joseph lived alone with his father, who was receiving welfare assistance but failed to provide him with deodorant, shampoo, laundry detergent, or money to use at the Laundromat. Joseph was only trying to be clean but was actually making his smell worse. It was difficult for him to attend school under these conditions, but he knew he needed an education if he was going to rise above his present situation.

Some teachers provided him with personal grooming needs and a second set of clothes, so he could wear one set while the other dried.

* * * * *

I volunteered to take a mother of six to the grocery store. She was living in a housing project on government assistance. The cost of a taxi cab to get to and from a grocery store used up too much of the family's budget. She was a caring, loving mother with little education.

The mother filled her grocery cart with bacon, chips, frozen novelties, snack cakes, and soft drinks. Everything was in individual serving

84

containers, and nothing took more cooking than what could be done in a simple frying pan.

She spent far too much money for far too little nutrition.

* * * * *

I asked Ronda why she didn't live with her siblings. One lived with her grandmother, one with an aunt, and one with her mother. She told me that it was because the aunt and grandmother had no children of their own in their homes; so this way, all three would qualify for government assistance as the head of a household with a child. Ronda said this was okay with her because they all lived on the same block and got to see each other all the time.

* * * * *

It is obvious to nearly everyone that our current system of helping those in need does not work. When we reward pregnant teenagers with money and special programs, it should be no surprise that we get many more pregnant teenagers.

Adults should quit saying early sex is an indication children are growing up too fast, because it really indicates just the opposite. We should actually be telling youths early sex is a sign of immaturity.

Receiving government aid should not be a consideration which influences life-style decisions of when or if to marry or have and rear children.

Giving checks or food stamps to parents does not guarantee that children will have even their basic needs met; nor will simply taking the parents off the welfare rolls after a specified period of time ensure that all of America's children will have proper food and clothing.

We need to expand the school's use in making sure that no American child goes hungry. The use of schools as delivery points of goods and services makes sense because the schools already provide some free meals and the buildings already exist, thus reducing the need for taxpayers to build new facilities.

School-age children are already served free breakfast and lunch five days a week if their family is in poverty, even though the family is often provided with food stamps to cover these same meals. However, these are not enough.

Poor children also need to be provided a cold sack dinner to be taken home at the end of the school day for their evening meal to ensure that no child in America goes to bed hungry.

Furthermore, Saturdays the school cafeteria area could be opened for four to six hours at which time poor families and the elderly could pick up needed food supplies, cleaning and personal hygiene products, clothing, and modest medical supplies (antiseptics, Band-Aids, burn creams, etc.).

According to this plan, even if parents refuse to work after expiration of welfare time limits, which are currently being imposed, children could still get these basic supplies on Saturdays. However, their non-working parents would not have access to salable food stamps or money.

If it sounds cruel and heartless to ask people in need to come once a week to the closest neighborhood school to get "hand outs," it is less cruel than the current system of food stamps in which many children needlessly suffer because their parents fail to follow through appropriately due to ignorance or neglect. This proposed plan would ensure good nutrition by directly providing easy access to a well-balanced choice of foods, which would be less likely than food stamps to be sold for other things. Rickets, motley skin, and lack of vigor from poor nutrition should not happen in America!

The concern about embarrassment from people having to go get these items is not nearly as important as our making sure basic needs of the poor are met. It is even more embarrassing, uncomfortable, and life-stunting to be without socks in the snow, proper food to eat, or medicine to put on an injury.

Many fine citizens have been reared in poverty. Cold bread and margarine sandwiches for lunch and hand-me-down clothes have been part of many successful, happy peoples' childhoods. We need to help children learn that there is no shame in the lack of money or material goods, nor should there be haughtiness in having material possessions.

How sad when people define their worth as an individual in terms of their material possessions! Children who think this way do so only because we adults lead them in this direction. America needs to stress the inner soul rather than the outside packaging.

Picking up food, personal grooming supplies, and household cleaning materials on Saturday should be no more embarrassing than making purchases with food stamps or trustees' vouchers, and it does provide a more secure safety net for children in need.

*****

Rollins' minor cuts became infected, requiring hospital treatment because his home didn't have common household medications.

*****

Tavel was leaning against my door on Monday morning. When I asked him how his weekend had been he said his little sister had died the day before. She had been sick for about a week, then died of a high fever.

His mother didn't own a thermometer and so couldn't monitor the baby's temperature.

*****

Roselyn's baby was crying all the time because she was teething. Roselyn's grandmother used a razor blade to cut off the baby's gums, thereby exposing the infant's teeth and getting the pain over all at once--instead of having the baby cry for weeks.

Unfortunately, without gums Roselyn's child had little chance of keeping her teeth.

*****

Wendy brought her six-month-old baby to show me at school. The baby's mouth and lower face was covered with sores. The baby was taken for medical treatment for venereal disease contracted from a male family member. Wendy had not known where to turn for help for her child.

* * * * *

These last anecdotes show an additional need: During Saturday hours for food and clothing distribution there also could be a time for quick check-ups from a medical doctor or nurse practitioner. Minor ailments could be treated and serious problems would be referred elsewhere. Just having someone give advice or making sure a health problem is not serious would be very beneficial.

We believe this proposed plan would deliver needed goods and services more directly with greater efficiency and cost effectiveness than current programs. However, the important point is not whether this or other subsistence programs save money or even cost a bit more: What is important is that the right messages are sent and the right help reaches our children.

BAD MESSAGES

Young people hear what we really say, so we need to be very careful what kind of messages we send. Even when they turn from us and seem resistive to the adult world, they are learning from our messages. We think we say don't use drugs, alcohol, or have sex. Then we have a rich and famous person--an actor or athlete--stand in front of a group of students and tell how he used drugs, drank, and had wild sex for years; and now, of course, he is sorry and hopes the audience won't do the same. What the audience hears is *"I'm rich, I'm successful, I'm up on this stage being applauded, and I did all these wild things in my youth--so it didn't really hurt me (it may have helped)--after all, we aren't applauding people who lived straight lives, are we? Besides, I quit when I wanted to; so can you."*

* * * * *

I stood in the back of one of these anti-drug programs, caringly paid for by the city's largest corporation, to judge the students' reactions. They listened intently as the man told of arrests and jail time for early marijuana use and selling, and then his move into smuggling cocaine for a multi-millionaire. He described the high life style of

91

riches connected with this--and gave the excuse that he really didn't know what was on the plane he flew. When caught he pleaded guilty, but he told the students he was really innocent, since he was being used by a rich man and the system.

While he said he didn't like jail, he used the five years of free time to read, learn, write a book, and develop his muscles in the weight room-- without ever giving up on his dreams. And when he was released he was in fact hired into an exciting media-related dream job--and he hasn't used illegal drugs since.

The students listened and were impressed. Comments I overheard were "He has lived an exciting life." "He's great." "I hope I get to do great things like that."

His life certainly seemed more rewarding than the lives of the non-drug traffickers they had seen.

* * * * *

VOUCHERS

Vouchers are being touted by many as the way to improve our schools. According to this plan, parents of school-age children would be given vouchers for thousands of dollars which they could give to any school that would accept their child.

At face value the voucher proposal sounds like a great idea; however, it is based on the faulty assumption that there are bad schools that exist apart from their clientele (parents and students). The problems that schools have are a reflection of the needs and behaviors of the student body. Moving students to a new area will not cure the students' problems; the problems will just be spread to a new area.

The horrifying outcome of the voucher system would be the breakdown of a shared cultural community in America--and without this we won't have a unified country.

Small schools would spring up in basements, churches, old factories, and closed strip malls all over the country. Some of these schools would be truly dedicated to teaching children; some would open just to get the voucher money; and, scarily, some would open to indoctrinate impressionable young minds.

Right-wing reactionaries, left-wing radicals, black militants, white supremacists, neo-nazis, and various cults would be paid taxpayer dollars to indoctrinate our youth. Young armies of dissenters would spring up. It is not acceptable for parents to be allowed to choose the ideology they want for their children, and then demand that society pay for it. Parents can be fooled or mislead themselves, and some can even be extremists.

Although under attack for being too leftist and humanistic, the public schools have enough variety in teachers and staff to keep things from getting too extreme. Public schools are a reflection of the community's needs and can be mandated to change at the voters' will--but this is not so of private schools.

Many private schools do a good job of filling a needed educational niche; however, the percentage of students in private schools is too small to affect the overall community. Parents whose children now attend these schools think they want the voucher program to become law so that they can receive financial help. But in the long run, for the good of their children, they must support public schools. Whatever monetary gains result from vouchers will matter little to the future lives of their children and grandchildren if our society breaks down into suspicious, hostile camps, because large numbers of young people did not get to know each other in a common, shared, cultural community center like our public schools.

The dividing of our country into different ethnic, racial, religious, and ideological camps can lead to massive upheaval such as seen recently in Rwanda, Ireland, and Bosnia. Branch Davidians, Heaven's Gate, Jim Jones' Peoples' Temple, and the Ku Klux Klan are examples of groups who could claim education status and receive tax money through vouchers by starting their own schools. Weird schools would pop up like dandelions in the spring and be even harder to control.

If Catholic, Episcopal, and Jewish schools are allowed to accept school vouchers, so can Hare Krishnas, Satanists, witches, and those who deify crystal pyramids. If one religious group receives this tax money, all religious groups--no matter how strange to the average person--can qualify. If only non-religious based schools are allowed to accept vouchers, and this ruling would eliminate most prestigious private schools, the door would still be open for tax-funding of neo-nazis, socialists, racial hate groups, and other such radical schools.

There would be no way to separate which schools should or should not get tax support. Checklists such as number of computers, books in the library, hours of instruction, size of classrooms, number of restrooms, and number of fire escapes which might earn accreditation and licensing approval of a school will not get at the core of the instruction that is taking place when outside visitors are not present.

ROLE MODELS

We all know that a child's first and best role models are his or her parents.

However, it behooves all adults to try to be good role models for our children. Unfortunately, many adults are so concerned with being thought of as young, wild, hip, or "with it," that they don't provide mature role models for children. They brag of drug use, sexual exploits, and schemes, scams, and shady deals, rather than acting like wise, mature adults.

When adults envy and emulate youngsters, youths are left confused and floundering while trying to find the path toward true growth and knowledge. Adults owe it to themselves and to the generations that follow to grow up with wisdom, serenity, self-knowledge, and a well-thought-out philosophy of life. This is the role model all children need.

Some parents believe that their role in life is to be their child's friend. Most school children don't need another friend; they need a guiding parent.

* * * * *

Lee Ann sat giggling with her mother, Janice. Janice had been asked to come to school because of Lee Ann's cutting classes and acting up.

Lee Ann and Janice were dressed just alike-- short shorts, low-cut halters, lots of makeup, and "big hair." They were holding hands while laughing at me.

Janice said she had hated school and expected Lee Ann to hate school, too. They double-dated and did everything together. Lee Ann's mother even signed her out of school so they could go to the mall together during school hours.

* * * * *

Stephanie's mother was crying in my office. She said she wanted to be a good parent, but sixteen-year-old Stephanie was threatening to run away from home.

Her mother was so afraid of this black-mail gambit that she had allowed Stephanie's boyfriend to move into her home. She provided food and expenses for both of them, although neither worked or went regularly to school.

Stephanie's boyfriend wanted more space, so her mother moved her bed into the basement to live, *giving her daughter and boyfriend the rest of the house she paid for in which to party, drink, and smoke marijuana.*

I suggested to Stephanie's mother that she was her daughter's role model, and as such she should do what was right and moral. If Stephanie should run away, at least her mother could look in the mirror and tell herself that she had set a good example, and had done what she felt was right. If she allowed Stephanie to drink, use drugs, and have sex in her home, and bad things happened to Stephanie, she (the mother) would be blamed.

Stephanie did not run away under the new rules, but her boyfriend left her when the mother quit giving her money and the run of the house.

Stephanie had learned an important lesson.

* * * * *

Adults need to be strong and demonstrate good moral values for their children. Although parents who do so might not be viewed as being "cool," eventually their children will admire and respect them for this.

Even if their children strongly disagree with parental guidance based on sound moral judgment,

99

when they reach maturity they will be glad their parents took a stand. Even if their children persist in ignoring sound advice, parents can at least look in the mirror years later and tell themselves--and tell their children--"I tried to be a good role model--I tried to lead you down the right path." Every parent owes this to his children--and to himself.

EMPHASIZING THE PAST

School children are often given the assignment to interview older family members and trace their ancestors. Such homework seems harmless and pleasant and allows students of all ages to trace their roots so as to better understand themselves. This activity is so popular that most students will have this same assignment given to them a number of times during their school career.

But what does all of this looking backwards really mean? While this information might be quite interesting, exactly how should students use it to shape their lives? Are we such a dying nation that our children's eyes must be focused on the past, rather than the future?

We are not saying to lessen the importance of traditional history, which needs even more classroom time. It is the emphasis on individual history that is the problem.

America was founded on the principle that each man stood for himself and had a chance to make as much of himself as he could, regardless of family history. Yes, we know that men of many races and all women were not included in this vision in the beginning, but all Americans are so included now.

In America it should not matter if your great grandfather was a prince, a holy man, a thief, or a murderer. What counts is the kind of life each individual chooses for himself.

School children frequently ask me about this topic. They are concerned that they somehow will end up the same as their relatives, some of whom have negative behaviors. They have heard that family patterns tend to repeat themselves in each new generation; for example, that abused children grow up to be abusers.

They are happy to learn that such negative behavioral patterns need not recur. Many neglected and abused people grow up to be the most empathetic, kind, and charitable of people. Some people from rich, doting families become self-centered egotists, and some do not.

It isn't easy for students to learn about themselves by looking backwards because the influence of their forefathers' lives on their present and future situations is often unclear; thus this assignment just confuses students. It would be better to have them write about the type of parent, grandparent, or citizen that they want to become in the future.

Personalizing history and trying to remediate past wrongs in the present lead to needless current divisiveness and tensions between people. What happened to your ancestors did not happen to you and cannot be changed. Schools need to stop emphasizing the personalization of history which serves to divide the American people into separate and opposing camps.

History is like a mosaic: To properly study it you need to gather as many pieces as possible and fit them together carefully. Even when done the best way possible, the cracks and missing pieces leave the picture less than completely accurate.

To have school children to find one small tile from their own roots and use this to develop an entire theory of the historical past gives them a very distorted view of history and often fosters the development of personalized, emotional responses.

REWARDS AND INCENTIVES

Why do you brush your teeth every day? To get that clean feeling, so your breath doesn't offend, so that your teeth don't decay, hurt, or eventually fall out? Or to earn a silver star on a chart that you can redeem for cash or prizes?

Many children today are rewarded for everything they do. Toilets play music when they aim correctly, parents give stars for routine household chores, libraries give hamburger coupons for pleasure reading, and schools give pizza parties for attending class.

Unfortunately, these reinforcers are ironically causing a decline in the very activities parents are trying to encourage.

This reward theory is based on the work/paycheck concept. It is true that most of us would not continue our jobs if our pay stopped. But many things we do--hobbies, sports, reading, cooking, cleaning, attending church--are not done for monetary or substantive gain.

Children need to learn to act correctly and accomplish tasks for intrinsic reasons. We clean our homes so we don't live in filth and disease. We eat well-balanced meals for health. We study so as not to be ignorant, and we have a moral code we abide by so we can live together in harmony. Nature has a way of punishing folks who follow no rules, even if society doesn't choose to do so--and children need to be taught this reality.

Rewarding positive behaviors with material products doesn't work for long. Children simply keep upping the ante until the adults can no longer continue the game. And the child feels cheated and angry because the rules suddenly changed.

* * * * *

A conference was held for fourteen-year-old Jason because of disruptive behavior at school. A psychologist, teachers, the parents, and Jason himself attended the meeting.

The mother begged her son to tell her what she could do to make him stay out of trouble. He said, "Buy me a motorcycle."

That he was legally too young to drive one made no difference to him. His mother cried and whined and offered other bribes but didn't furnish him with a motorcycle.

Her son became sullen and continued to act out in school.

* * * * *

Giving a child candy to write spelling words only works until the candy stops coming or he has had his fill of sweets.

Even when a parent is able to provide continuously escalating rewards and incentives, he needs to carefully consider the message that is given.

* * * * *

Michael was given a car, insurance, and gas to encourage good grades in math. For a while this worked: He brought his advanced algebra grade up to an "A," and his family was proud.

One night he had a few (illegal) beers behind a mall and crashed his car into a very large trash dumpster. Nobody was hurt; the police didn't arrest anyone, but the car would no longer run.

Michael's next grade report was bad and included an "F" in algebra. When I talked with him he was adamant that he would begin to study only when his parents purchased a new car for him, and they were being too slow in doing so.

I explained to Michael that he studied so as not to be ignorant, to earn a high school diploma, and perhaps to get in the Coast Guard, his personal goal at that time. Studying math--or not studying math--should have nothing to do with either having or not having a car.

* * * * *

We don't attend school to get pizzas. We are not good citizens to earn "merit" T-shirts. We do not wash our hands before meals to get a stuffed teddy bear. Teaching children to crave rewards and incentives for performing life's necessary duties is cheating the children out of self-satisfaction, understanding of primary responsibilities, and delayed gratification.

TIME IN SCHOOL

A major predictor of school success is attendance. Students who aren't in class can't be taught by even the best teachers.

Lengthening the hours schools are in session each year has been widely proposed as a way for U.S. students to do better in international achievement comparisons. However, longer school days and longer school years will not help underachieving students if they don't attend. This is an expensive endeavor that is doomed because most failing students miss over fifteen per cent of the school days now scheduled. They would simply miss more days if more were scheduled and nothing else changed.

Students who now attend school regularly and are taking challenging classes are on par with their international counterparts; it is the school truants and slackers who are bringing our averages down.

Truancy begins in grade school for some students. Parents move from place to place, hide out from bill collectors and jealous boyfriends, and just simply don't bother to get up in the mornings to get their children ready for school.

* * * * *

Lana said she had a seven-year-old sister who stayed in a closet for most of the day and had not been outside the home for two years.

Her mother sold and used cocaine and prostituted from the home and had not bothered to purchase any new clothing to fit her younger daughter for more than a year. Since the girl had outgrown her old clothes and had nothing to wear, she couldn't leave the house.

The mother had never enrolled her younger daughter in any school, so the authorities didn't know she existed. The police went to the home the same day I made the report and found a naked little girl with delayed development. Mother and boyfriend apparently left town, but the two sisters were happily placed with an out-of-town grandmother.

Meanwhile, the school copes with the child's struggle to grasp basic material. This is an unusually sad, but unfortunately not too uncommon case.

* * * * *

Many parents keep young children home day after day because they are too lazy to send them to school. Older children are often kept at home to baby-sit and do laundry. (The popularity of the staying-home-to-do-laundry excuse through the years amazes me.)

Older children begin to miss school of their own volition around the sixth grade, and the problem steadily gets worse with age. Instead of being in the classroom receiving the instruction that taxes have paid for, they stay home to watch TV, sleep late, and be with friends. When informed of attendance problems, and when issued failing report cards for their children, parents often claim they can do nothing to make their children attend school. The child who does not attend school is doomed to failure. Increasing the school year will not change this situation.

Attendance rewards and incentives from the school help a few students. Parents who will work with the school on a contingency reinforcement plan of positive rewards for school attendance (and consequences for nonattendance) can help even more students stay in school. In some difficult cases, parents who help children break mandatory attendance laws might even be jailed, but there is a reluctance to jail mothers and fathers who need to maintain homes and provide child care; so this technique is seldom used.

A useful approach to this widespread problem of lackadaisical school attendance would be to attach financial gains and losses to school attendance. Taxpayers' money is wasted when children don't attend school. The community and society as a whole suffers when children fail to learn to become responsible citizens. The taxpaying community has a stake in enforcing school attendance. Parents must be held responsible for ensuring their children's school attendance.

At the present time we basically "pay" parents to rear their children. Welfare, ADC, SSI, WIC, and other programs are all in place because taxpayers want better futures for today's children. (Food stamps, housing assistance, and Medicare/Medicaid exist to help people survive in the here and now.) Parents not on public assistance can get tax breaks and tax credits to help pay for child rearing.

We need to tie these financial benefits with school attendance. Children who do not attend school at least ninety per cent of the time would lose tax credits, and parents on public assistance would lose part of that money. This approach is different from some current programs which require school enrollment rather than attendance.

This plan would add some cost and paper work to our bureaucracies, but the final cost of doing nothing about attendance problems is far too high.

Each school, public or private, would issue a type of "W-2 Form" stating student attendance to be attached to the parents' tax forms. Home school children would get a form from the state verifying that the parents had complied with the individual state's home schooling requirements to send in with their taxes. Public assistance agencies would also require such paper work.

Only documented medical statements could over-ride this attendance requirement, and even then most seriously ill children are educated with school-provided homebound or hospital teachers and so are considered as attending school. Juveniles in detention centers are also provided with teachers so they may continue their education. Therefore, all parents would have access to student attendance verification or a licensed medical doctor's statement.

Is it fair to hold parents responsible for their children's school attendance? Yes. They are in a better position than anyone else to control their children with rewards and punishments.

Parents can also attend school with their child if necessary. Many times just the threat of mom or dad sitting beside them in class is enough to improve the student's behavior and attendance. (Unfortunately, many parents are more willing to accept school failure than to take such action.) On some occasions, I've arranged for a parent to spend an entire day sitting right beside his child. One day of this with the threat of others like it--if cutting continues--usually cures the problem. Most schools will welcome parents to watch their child in action during the school day.

SAYING NO TO DRUGS

If we want students to avoid using drugs we need to show them how down-trodden, ugly, and used up they are likely to become with continued drug usage. Showing them that drugs will make them weak, wimpy, and sick will have more impact on future behaviors than showing glowingly successful ex-drug users.

Youth thinks it is invincible, and death is so remote that examples of blackened lungs and crashed cars with dead bodies mean nothing. However, teens do care about physical appearance. The best non-smoking technique I've ever used was showing wrinkled faces of smokers as compared to non-smokers the same age. For drinking I stress they could end up impotent and mentally incompetent, and that drug use might wreck their brains until they can't drive a car.

Relating illicit behaviors to things teens really value--attractiveness, sexuality, and driving a car--can be very effective.

114

GANGS

Gang membership is not optional to young people living in certain locales. They must either become members or victims with damaged lives resulting from either choice. When big-name journalists and social scientists claim that the only solution to gang membership is to get at the root causes--poverty, institutionalized racism, and inequality of opportunity in our country--this is of scant help to families who must now live in areas dominated by gangs.

Saving one child at a time may be the best people in the trenches can accomplish while others debate the larger issues of American society.

An example is a fourteen-year-old whose family recently had moved into a gang-run area. He was beaten up and scared into joining. When he came to me, he had already been branded on the chest--his life-long membership card. He had been ritualistically initiated and forced to participate in his first major criminal act. He was a scared and scarred young man, but his mother and step-father knew nothing of any of this.

The family could not run away, but after their initial shock when I told them of the problem, they agreed to devote some time to saving their son.

The plan was simple but effective: I watched over him at school (not hard since it entailed his going to classes and staying in assigned areas with no deviations), and his mother or step-father watched over him at home. When the phone rang, one of them answered and said he was on restriction and couldn't use the phone. When gang members came to the home to get him, the step-father said the son was grounded and couldn't leave the house. Weekends he went to his grandmother's house when he wasn't with his parents.

This plan worked. The gang got tired of coming for him to no avail and surprisingly seemed to respect the concept of parental control and discipline.

The way to save many children from gangs is to use the small group method. Starting when children are very young parents, grandparents, and neighbors need to devote time to watching the children. Parents can get together and agree that whenever their children are playing an adult will watch over them. A simple old-fashioned idea--but one that would help many children--is adult supervision at all times. This may seem like a burden to overworked parents and horrifyingly restrictive to teenagers, but the price for free time in a gang community is much, much higher.

Grade schools could have anti-gang meetings. Parents could get to know each other well enough to work out play schedules and fun times for the youngsters before the gangs get to them. Parents could explain to the children that it is better to have a few good friends than being part of a large group leading them astray.

The schools and churches cannot take the place of this family-watch. When one large, urban church opened its doors to teen dances and parties it quickly became a hang-out and recruiting place for gangs. After several large fights between rival gangs which injured people, the church was forced to close down the program.

For profit under twenty-one clubs have many of the same problems and more. They become preying grounds for adults seeking young sexual company. Parents and grandparents drop children off at these places thinking that they are in a safe, wholesome environment--but I hear about the sexual molestations, knife fights in the alley, and undercover drug sales the next day.

Even dropping off unsupervised teens at the local mall may not be safe.

* * * * *

A handcuffed youth once bragged to me about his involvement with a gang shooting outside the mall the previous night while we waited for the paddy wagon to take him to jail.

His middle-class mother cried and said she couldn't believe that this could happen since she herself drove him to a nice, clean mall nearly every night after dinner, and his friends brought him home by eleven o'clock each night.

I wondered what she thought he was doing for five hours each night--trying on new outfits with his friends?

* * * * *

While parents should not be overly suspicious, they should be realistic regarding what may happen to their children. They should make a point of showing up unexpectedly at under twenty-one clubs, dances, parties, and malls to see for themselves what their children are doing. Parents should not rely on third-person reports, which can be very misleading.

Visible police crack downs on gang violence and drug dealing can also send a message to young gang "wannabes." Parents and the community need to support the police in this effort to stop the flow of lost children.

Many older adults are financially profiting by using young gang members. Their gold-wheeled fancy cars and multiple gold chains are appealing. They also need to be targeted for arrest when they break the law.

Affluent suburban communities as well as urban areas have gang problems, although perhaps not yet as severe. Suburban parents need to use the same family-watch method for their children, by supervising activities and popping up on surprise visits to check on their children.

These are especially important in homes where everyone works during the day. Locations of party houses are circulated between students. All it takes to become a party house is the knowledge that no parent will be at home. This gives students a safe place to cut classes, watch TV, drink beer, or have sex. Some party houses are used for a long time. The child who lives there cleans up and hides the evidence before the unsuspecting adult returns.

Other party houses are rapidly trashed. They are good for one use only.

* * * * *

One mother came home from work to find her carpet stained, her sofa ripped, her toilet clogged, and the kitchen nearly unusable. She asked the school to deal with the matter because she didn't want to call the police (as the school had advised).

She wanted all of the students involved except her own child expelled from school because her daughter had told the others not to damage things, but the twenty-five or so friends who accepted her invitation to the house hadn't minded her.

The school suspended all the students-- including her daughter--for cutting classes, displeasing the parent again.

* * * * *

After-school time alone at home is often used as a time for drugs, drinking, or sex. Again, it is the knowledge of no adult supervision for a specific period of time that allows freedom for these activities.

Of course, all parents can't quit their jobs to stay home to watch their children, and live-in grandmothers and neighbors you can count on to tell you who came to your home are not always available. But parents can take away the knowledge of a safe haven for illicit behaviors and truancy by telling their children that they love them and care for them and so will be coming by the house at unexpected times.

Parents should take a lunch hour at 10:30 or 2:30 occasionally, and eat at home. Vacation time or compensatory time sometimes can be used by the hour for early home arrivals or unexpected visits at home during various times of the day a few times a year. Aunts, uncles, and grandparents can stop by the home whenever they can to see if everything is all right. In the summer teens left alone can be surprised with brunches, lunches, or shopping trips by family members with a free hour or so.

The whole point is the randomness of the visits. If a child never knows when an adult might pop in, he is less tempted to misbehave, and your home is less likely to be misused by others seeking a den of iniquity.

THE BIG LIE

You can tell a lot about a civilization's values by looking at the huge edifices they build--whether pyramids for the king's afterlife, temples to worship sun gods, stone monuments to human sacrifice, coliseums for bloody battles, fabulous art museums, or massive cathedrals to preach humanity toward mankind.

Our society uses tax dollars to build huge sports arenas in which richly paid athletes are cheered and applauded. We teach our youth to glorify the ability to run, jump, throw, kick, and hit a ball more than the ability to heal, teach, build, or preach.

The respect and pay society is willing to give to various types of work is topsy-turvy. Work that is most important for people to live together safely, ensuring we have clean water, sewer sanitation, trash pick-up, food delivery, heat, and shelter maintenance, gets little respect and meager financial reward.

The least important activities--dropping a ball through a net, kicking it over a post, or putting it into a hole, none of which accomplishes anything of lasting value--are held in high esteem and are handsomely rewarded financially.

Is it any wonder that our children spend countless hours bouncing balls, watching sports, and day-dreaming that they will some day reach this pinnacle of success, rather than reading, studying, or doing hundreds of other activities?

It is not only a big lie to tell our youth that the way to achieve riches and fame is through sports, since the percentage of those who make it to the top is infinitesimally small. It is also a lie to tell our youth that sports, in and of themselves, have any lasting value for civilization or for the advancement of the human soul or spirit.

Sports are wonderful for helping in the maintenance of a healthy body and for the momentary pleasure of a game, but the idolization of sports has gone too far.

* * * * *

One city high school strapped for cash called a meeting for all teachers to tell them there was no money for paper. Backsides of used paper and odd-colored lots had been depleted, and teachers were on their own to figure out a way to make do until the end of the school year.

However, at the same meeting teachers were told the new seven million dollar second gym (the first gym was still quite functional) being built onto that same school was progressing nicely.

The same school had no reading teacher that year, but did increase its number of paid coaches.

* * * * *

Not only immature school children dream of gaining riches through sports: Their parents and taxpayers keep pushing money into sports and away from other sorts of societal development.

* * * * *

A Mayor of a major midwest city recently suggested library patrons pay some "user fees" to support the public libraries, instead of approving additional funding for expansion of needed services.

The irony of this suggestion was that the same city Mayor had recently built a fabulous new baseball field for the city, approved tax monies to be raised for an improved basketball arena, and was in the process of finalizing a new multi-million dollar tax program to keep a professional football team from leaving town.

If you were a child in this city, wouldn't you think that playing with balls is more important than reading and learning?

FAIR AND EQUAL

The quest to be fair and equal above all other goals is an ill-fated one for our schools.

Life is naturally not fair. I am very fond of all shades of blue, and so nearly each day I get a sky filled with my favorite color. This is, of course, unfair to anyone whose favorite color is lime green or scarlet, who may feel bitter about my seeing the color I love fill the sky all over the world, while his favorite color never gets a chance.

This pursuit of artificial equality has started a downward spiral toward the lowest common denominator. The removal of competition and individual creativity stifles high achievement. The advent of cooperative learning with its emphasis on group projects and group grades has frustrated the high achievers as it raises lower achievers' grades.

It is necessary for people to learn to work together in groups, and so some school time spent in group projects can be beneficial for all students; but much of our country's growth and development sprang from innovative loners. True leaps in human knowledge tend to come from individual efforts, rather than committees.

In fact, most well-functioning "work-place" groups are really individuals with specific tasks to perform, who bring their individual components together to complete a project, rather than the entire group working on the overall project. Real-world projects also have leaders to guide the others and competition both inside and outside the group for recognition, status, and success. To try to eliminate such intrinsic motivators from the school setting is futile and does little to prepare students for the future.

Bitterness, frustration, and anger can be the outcome for high achievers when assigned only group grades and projects. Lower-achieving students learn to expect others to take care of them with minimal effort on their part.

The quest for sameness or equality is now pervasive. We should all have equal material goods, regardless of effort; we should all have equal access to various careers, despite natural abilities. Perhaps a national lottery could be held, assigning people college admittance and career placement.

We now have teachers who can't read with classroom assistants hired to teach reading skills, doctors who can't see with assistants hired to describe visual symptoms--all in the effort to not recognize individual skills and aptitudes, and to give everyone an equal chance at everything.

An outer suburban school system decided to enhance its educational image and improve property values by declaring itself an all honor achievement school system: All students attending their schools were honor roll students, and all their staff taught so well that every student achieved grades of *"A"* or *"B."*

This was a quickly-achieved goal as teachers were permitted to only give grades of *"A"* or *"B"* on grade report cards.

Every parent could proudly display a "My child is an honor roll student" bumper sticker, and student competition was relaxed. If a family moved away, their children took honor grade transcripts to new schools. Families who moved in knew that report cards would look good when Xeroxed to grandma. But such artificially-induced equality of grades blurs the strengths and weaknesses both between people and, just as importantly, within an individual; so self-knowledge of individual aptitudes and trust in others' skills decline.

Our national quest for sameness is even apparent in our physical appearance: A great deal of money is spent each year on braces to give all children the same smile as their peers. Small breasts are made larger; large breasts are made smaller. Curly hair is straightened; straight hair is curled. Parents of short children beg medical doctors for medication to make them taller.

We need to face the truth: All things cannot be fair and equal by the very nature of life itself.

* * * * *

A presentation by a nationally-known motivational speaker informed students that they could do and be anything in the world they wanted in life.

Afterwards, one of my students asked me if I thought what the presenter had said was true. I said "No. Life is like a deli line. There are lots of choices for everyone, but if your heart is set on the last piece of Dutch apple pie the guy in front of you got--and you won't consider lemon, banana, chocolate, or peach pie, or the other forty-seven dessert choices available--you could end up empty-handed, resentful, and unhappy."

The boy smiled: He didn't believe the speaker, either.

* * * * *

129

Everybody has a great many pathways from which to choose in life. In fact, the number of choices and opportunities we each have is nearly overwhelming, even if it is not infinite.

MEDIA

No consideration of the problems of today's schools could leave out the share of blame which belongs to popular media.

The mixing of sex, violence, and humor together cheapens life's experiences for developing minds.

Whether or not viewing media violence can actually cause violent behavior is still being researched, but one thing is very clear: Young people think that they should use TV shows, commercials, print ads, and music as models for real-life behavior. They long to look and act like the media stars they glorify, and the messages they are receiving are the very antithesis of being good, caring citizens.

Although many observers deplore the impact that wholesale sex and violence have upon our youth, we are particularly concerned about the values portrayed on TV: The smart remark, the put-down to adults, trashy, sexy dress, vulgar language, extreme emphasis on materialism, disregard for others' needs, and lack of delayed gratification that are frequently shown on television. Although less sensational than sex and violence, the constant portrayal of examples such as these might be more harmful in the long run by turning us into a less caring, ruder, more self-absorbed society.

Commercials are especially damaging because they are carefully designed and packaged to be loud, attention-getting, and easily remembered. The ad people may think they are selling a cologne or a soft drink, but they are using psychological ad techniques honed to perfection over the years to impress questionable behaviors on gullible young minds.

How many commercials do you see which teach respect for adults, good citizenship, kindness for all, and values beyond the superficial?

TEACHING THINKING SKILLS

Too many school systems have swallowed the high-tech notion that children need to know only how to "source" information, rather than to really read and understand new material.

Many students are satisfied if they can locate topics on the internet which are only distantly related to their assignments. Pages of school reports are then printed out without the student having to actually read or learn anything. This activity is much easier than the old time method of actually hand-copying an encyclopedia entry.

Education started on this downward slope long ago when calculators entered the classroom. Why learn math facts when a cheap, hand-held calculator could do it quickly?

Then came the reluctance to learn the math theory behind the calculations. Now I must teach older students how to estimate appropriate math answers using arithmetic. Otherwise, they press buttons on the calculator and accept a checkbook balance of $72,943,016.76, if that is what the calculator says.

Thinking skills are wonderful to have. However, people first must have knowledge in order to have something to think about. Without in-depth studying of art, history, science, and so forth, people can't use thinking skills effectively, and only come up with ideas as deep as the shallow thoughts of the average TV talk show guest.

The hard fact that students must face is that they need to read and learn about a lot of things if they are to become knowledgeable adults. This country already has enough people willing to tell what they think without first bothering to learn anything.

The most valuable thinking-skills activity we can give students is how to do classical debating, which emphasizes research, timing rules, and most importantly, non-self-selected topic stances. Such activities help students understand both (or several) sides of an issue as well as the manner and techniques of presenting ideas and concepts to others.

COUNSELING YOUNG OFFENDERS IN SCHOOL

Some youths can be effectively helped within the school setting.

*****

I counseled a youth, Wendel, who was returned to school after incarceration for attempted murder.

At first, Wendel declared his innocence of wrong-doing because he only did what he felt he had to do. He felt justified in his behavior since the situation had given him no other choices.

We went over the details which had led to his arrest slowly, point by point, a number of times. In the beginning sessions, I listened to his story from his point of view. Then we went over his actions again, each time stopping where he could have made another decision that would have led to a different outcome--letting him think of what else he could have done at each juncture that led to his crime.

Slowly Wendel began to see that he did have some control over his life, that he made choices

135

which led to specific outcomes, and that he had the power to make some changes in his life, if he so desired.

Wendel had put on his heavy gold chain at 11:30 p.m. on a Tuesday night to "see what was up" behind a boarded-up car wash.

I later explained that he had chosen to go out late at night on a school night to a place where trouble-makers routinely hung out; that he chose to wear his fancy, tempting gold; and that he had even chosen to spend a great deal of money on gold when, as a child on welfare, he could have saved for a better future.

During the incident he was robbed of his necklace by two youths with a knife. Instead of calling the police, he decided to take care of this problem himself. At fifteen he felt it would be better not to have adult involvement.

Wendel went to his friend's grandmother's apartment, where he knew a gun was kept, and chose to pay for its rental. Then he went hunting for two days for the youths with only the nickname of one for a clue. He found them, chose to shoot at them, and was very angry that the gun was "no good" because he missed one and only slightly wounded the other.

Police did get involved at this point. Wendel served time and never got his gold chain back.

When he returned to school, he was still focused on revenge for the gold necklace. After a lot of counseling hours, Wendel finally began to understand that many of his troubles were because of decisions he could control. He eventually began making passing grades, began to accept responsibility for the choices he made, and began to plan for his future.

* * * * *

Many of my violent students see no other choices than acting out their anger and frustrations. They think they "have a temper" much the way they have five fingers instead of six on each hand. Nothing can be done about it; or they think the world leaves them no other choice but fighting and violent behavior.

Two techniques have been very successful with acting out students. The first, as shown in the example about Wendel, is making them understand that they have alternative behaviors at their command which can lead to different outcomes.

National Starch, a business located in my community, generously gave me two thousand dollars for a conflict resolution program. I purchased a television, video player, and camcorder. A day or so after the purchase a fight occurred. When calmness was restored, I had students to act out for the camera exactly what had occurred to cause the problem.

We tried to re-enact the dialogue and action as exactly as possible. The students loved this experience and especially enjoyed seeing themselves perform. (They would never give as much attention even to a well-known face as they did their own!)

Then we replayed the video, stopping the tape at critical junctures to discuss different responses and actions that could have been taken by the participants. Finally, we reshot the whole episode using different responses for a non-violent outcome. This remake allowed the students to role play and practice making more positive behavioral choices. Their sense of humor about themselves and awareness of tone of voice and body language all made this a positive learning experience.

After listening to the tape, one girl exclaimed, "I didn't know I sounded like that" (sarcastic and belligerent). A week later she told me she got into less fights because now she knew to talk nicer when asking for something.

Another successful technique makes students aware of their own body reactions and their control over them. First, I've helped students become aware of their own physical responses to anger and fear. Some clinch their fists, others tighten jaw muscles, or pop their knuckles, or change their breathing rate.

Everyone has a particular, overt, physical reaction to stress. Once a particular student's stress reaction is discovered, he is taught to counteract it. Children whose hands tense up are taught to stretch their fingers out very widely. Jaw clinchers learn to push front teeth slightly forward to relax facial muscles. Rapid breathers learn to breath slowly and deeply. Those who hold their breath too long learn to breathe at a normal rate.

I've had emotionally disturbed children who could not do these exercises on their own. I've had to do such things as stroke their hands and fingers to get them unclenched and relaxed, until they learn to do these actions themselves.

The relaxing of tense muscles and the return to normal breathing patterns give students a moment to think more calmly about their choice of behaviors. The very acts of relaxing muscles and controlling breathing serve to calm them to such an extent that the need to lash out at that moment is gone.

A useful caveat for teachers working with upset or potentially violent persons, whether students or parents: Keep people seated. For some reason that I do not fully understand, this simple act helps people to keep their emotions under control to a greater extent. If they refuse to sit down, you'd better take security measures because the potential for violence is much greater.

SHALLOW INSTRUCTION

I first saw integrated teaching in action twenty years ago in a single "show-case" fifth grade classroom. The students had spent most of the year studying Hawaii. They showed off the classroom mural they had painted, prepared Hawaiian food for us (canned pineapple and maraschino cherries), danced in grass skirts and leis, and had a wonderful time performing for parents and staff.

Unfortunately, this award-winning teacher had had to short-change teaching the fifth grade curriculum due to time spent on these fun projects, a problem that would be apparent to the sixth grade teacher. It was also apparent that these children had a misconception of our fiftieth state of Hawaii, and would be surprised to find airports, office buildings, and freeways there, instead of girls dressed in grass skirts.

Too much valuable learning time was spent learning one thing incorrectly.

Integrated teaching purports to teach many skills, such as math, English, reading, history, and so on, all wrapped up into one exciting package, often with a final project or portfolio as a result. Parents can then view the play, mural, dance, song, art

141

drawings, or whatever end item the group accomplishes. Students tend to love these classes and their parents are happy that they like school.

However, it behooves parents and others to look beyond the surface to make sure that depth of learning is taking place.

* * * * *

A mother of a suburban high school senior showed me with some delight a collage her daughter had made from cutting out magazine ads for her U.S. government project. It was colorful and pretty, but when her daughter flunked out of college the next year, I suspected a lack of study skills as the root of the problem.

* * * * *

Learning math, foreign language, science, and history takes effort, dedication, and systematic study which is not always exciting; however, neither is much of life, in which many of us must do unfulfilling work and other mundane activities which eventually make possible the achievement of higher goals.

Thus, the hard work and study of subjects such as those just mentioned will not only prepare students for life with their expanded knowledge, but will also teach them the ability to delay gratification, which will help them to become more responsible citizens.

ALWAYS ANOTHER CHANCE

Media, family, church, and school now send out the same message: No mistake is permanent. No matter what bad choices you make, you'll always get another chance.

There is no piper to be paid at the end of the dance. No behavior will really change your life or your soul.

Stories abound of young mothers who got GED's and now attend college on full, free grants while receiving free child care, housing, food, and medical assistance. Their smiling expectations of future careers and happiness contrast sharply with girls who remain chaste and attend college classes part time while paying their own ways with full-time waitressing jobs.

Maternity prom dresses are admired, and girls with babies are rewarded with double lunch periods so they can have more time to socialize together than non-parental teens. Students who don't do class work, cut classes, and misbehave expect and are routinely given multiple extra chances through summer school, night classes, alternative schools, independent work, and homebound teaching.

144

None of these extremely expensive options has led to a better-educated, more responsible citizenry. However, they have increased demands for unlimited chances at the expense of those who behave and perform within acceptable ranges and take responsibility for their behavior; and they have increased the very negative behaviors which have lowered the moral climate of our country.

* * * * *

Jason and his mother were highly indignant when he was refused another chance in school. Jason had been released from jail a week earlier to attend school when he flicked his Bic, setting a girl in front of him on fire. The school contended that this offense was very serious; the girl's hair gel was highly flammable, not to mention that he had violated the rule against having matches or lighters in school. (There is no written rule against setting students on fire.)

When the school asked for an expulsion, the mother claimed that having attended only five days of school did not give her son "a chance." I said he had only attended five days, and had already caused bodily harm. The compromise was his attendance in an expensive, easier, shorter, after-

hours program where we hoped he could control himself.

And Jason learned, once again, that someone else will smooth over his errors.

* * * * *

THE PURPOSE OF PUBLIC SCHOOL EDUCATION

What is the purpose of public schools? What are they to accomplish?

The reason that taxpayers have been willing to fund a public education for all of its people is to prepare competent, capable citizens, people who will vote responsibly, who can think, and who can act in a reasonable manner to keep society going for all of us.

We should not provide a public education just to turn out trained workers.

The value of the old liberal arts education has begun to fall by the wayside. This trend is a tragic mistake. A liberal arts education, one of philosophy, history, music, art, literature, and science enriches people so they can have a fuller life, be better citizens, better parents, and in totality make a better culture and country for everyone.

The emphasis on liberal arts education started to fall by the wayside as we began to emphasize the importance of educating people not to think, not to be good citizens, not to vote appropriately, but to earn a living. We began to think less of education and more of training.

An educated person knows a great deal about the world in general; this knowledge provides a basis for rejecting, manipulating, refining, or changing new information. In contrast, a training program teaches people how to perform a skill, rather than how to think and grow.

While training prepares us for jobs, education prepares us for life.

Several years ago our schools began to emphasize training at the requests of parents, the community in general, and future employers. Unfortunately, the schools are typically unable to adapt their training and equipment to the fast pace of technological change. The cost is just too much. As a result, a typical sophomore using four-year-old equipment in a classroom will be at least seven years behind when he applies for a job; thus retraining is required.

So not only have we taken much time and money from liberal arts instruction, but we also are unable to provide continuously-updated, state-of-the-art vocational training. The bottom line here is that precious educational time and dollars are being ineffectively utilized.

Businesses themselves should expect to train people to do the exact requirements of each job. If the schools would provide greater emphasis on a well-rounded liberal arts education, companies hiring our students would find that training them specific vocational skills would be easy.

Instead of building enormously-expensive career complexes, perhaps the emphasis should be shifted to part-time internships at real industrial settings. Everybody would win with such internships: The students would learn real-life job skills and expectations by means of on-the-job training at a real work site, with state of the art equipment--while earning money. Vocational educational teachers would serve as liaisons between the school and businesses, and provide student assistance as required.

The employer could train future employees exactly the way they need to function, would get to try out personnel before committing to hiring them, and would get work done for reduced rates. And the taxpayers would save tremendous money by not having to build very expensive, yet quickly outmoded, artificial training environments.

And schools could concentrate more heavily on what they do best--teaching liberal arts instruction which expands students' minds and encourages them to think.

RED HERRING

It is time for the quiet little secret about race to be exposed: There is no such thing as race as it is being used today to separate the U.S. population.

What is the proof of this statement? Just answer these questions: How many races are there? How many races were there in 1820 or 1950? Ask a Korean-American if he or she is of the same race as a Japanese-American. Is a Swedish-American the same race as an Italian-American or a Russian-American?

Racial divisions are culturally defined. As a result, they vary from country to country and even from one time period to another within the same country.

Neither a blood test nor any type of physical examination can definitively place a person into a racial category. And while many people base racial designation on more or less distinct physical characteristics, nothing--not skin color, nor hair texture, nor eye shape, nor height of cheek bone placement--is exclusively unique to one race or another.

Race is not a thing of nature, but a bigotry of man, and it is time for mankind to begin to abolish it, whether in the U.S., Japan, Rwanda, or Bosnia.

People are like dogs, who can all live together, mate, and produce young in a huge spectrum of shape, size, and color. We are not like birds, each of which can only nest and mate with its exact same kind. The world is filled with happy mutts; but no part-robin, part-hummingbird, part-cardinal exist in nature.

We do not deny the social, religious, cultural, and nationalistic differences that exist between individuals. Groups of people who live, work, and worship together often develop similar customs, beliefs, speech, and mannerisms. None of these differences changes the fact that there is just one human race.

So how does a school system establish the race of a student? In many cases it is simply whatever the student and the parent(s) declare. Racial designations have even been revised when parents have changed their minds.

Students know how to use the race issue very effectively so they won't be held accountable for their negative behavior, and to keep from growing in knowledge as quickly as they might. The cry of *prejudice* is expected to make all adults jump, and to, in effect, take the spot-light away from the youth and focus it elsewhere.

I personally have had a black child file a complaint with me about a white teacher's prejudice in her treatment of him. The teacher was very upset and nearly cried over the accusation. It turned out that the white teacher expected him to be in class, on time, with his book, listening, and not talking.

I have had a white child file a complaint with me about a black teacher's prejudicial treatment of her. The teacher was very upset and wrung her hands in concern over this accusation. It turned out the black teacher wanted her to be in class, on time, with her book, listening, and not talking.

* * * * *

Once I had a group of students come to complain about their teacher's prejudicial behavior toward them. I looked at the group of males and females, black and white students, and asked what sort of prejudice she was demonstrating.

They thought for awhile and then responded, "She's prejudiced against teenagers."

She wanted them in class, on time, sitting at their own computers, listening to her instructions.

* * * * *

Adults are too quick to respond to accusations of prejudice made by youngsters trying to get out of the hard work of becoming knowledgeable, responsible citizens.

We are not denying that prejudiced teachers occasionally exist; however, experience indicates that teachers are much more concerned about behavior than race. Whatever prejudicial thoughts teachers might have in their hearts, in day-to-day teaching they reward students who are enthusiastic, hard-working, and interested--regardless of their race. Conversely, they are equally likely to be frustrated by disobedient students--regardless of race.

SAFE HAVENS

With more and more parents being unwilling or unable to handle the day-to-day pressures of child-rearing, society needs to expand the options available for providing safe, caring places--safe havens--for children. The following anecdotes demonstrate the need for safe havens for children.

* * * * *

Nora's mother moved Saturday afternoon because she couldn't pay the overdue rent. Monday Nora told me that her mother had said she would be back to get her later Saturday night, but so far she hadn't returned.

She didn't know where her mother was now; the last she saw of her was in her mother's friend's truck with the furniture in the back as they left. Her mother had said there wasn't room for Nora in the truck.

I finally traced down her mother through numerous leads. Her mother claimed that she had gone back for her daughter that weekend but couldn't find her. Nora was returned to her mother and both received counseling through the schools.

* * * * *

Terry's mother's new boyfriend was tired of putting up with kids, so he and Terry's mother went to visit friends somewhere in Kentucky for awhile, leaving the children alone.

Terry and his siblings were placed in an over-crowded group home until the State Police could locate their mother.

* * * * *

Sherry's mother phoned me; she didn't want her fifteen-year-old daughter anymore. The girl was lazy, wouldn't do her chores, and talked back. She claimed she couldn't put up with the stress of rearing Sherry because she had high blood pressure. She wanted me to come get Sherry. She said "Take her any place. I'm just tired of her."

I told the mother there is no place to take a girl who doesn't do her chores. When the mother insisted she wouldn't keep her, I had the mother to call the police and tell them so they could explain the legalities of the situation.

* * * * *

Leon's mother used crack cocaine. Leon said, "Sometimes she takes off, and we don't see her for a day or more. And even when she's home we don't know what kind of mood she'll be in." He added that she's "much meaner and nastier when she can't get any crack."

The mother's participation in her four young children's lives was negligible. The children struggled on the best they could.

Leon said they all needed help, but he didn't want to get his mother into any more trouble.

* * * * *

Teresa said her mother and her mother's boyfriend fought all the time because they drank too much.

Neither adult worked, so they could stay up all hours drinking.

There were bullet holes in the walls and broken furniture to attest to the violence of their fights. Newspapers covered dirty, broken window panes, and the stuffing was coming out of ripped-up chairs.

Teresa called the police when the fights got out of hand. The police came and quieted them down for the night, but it started again the next day when the drinking began anew.

Teresa said she wished she didn't have to live there anymore.

* * * * *

For the past several years I have handled cases like these several times a week, and I'm just one of hundreds of case workers. We already have foster homes, group homes, runaway shelters, and emergency placement shelters for children, but there are not nearly enough of them. Many places are restricted to certain ages, handicapping conditions, gender, or time restrictions, and so cannot accommodate the variety of children who need safe places to stay.

There simply are not enough of these shelters for all the needy children, and overcrowding for those which exist is a serious problem.

New group homes need to be established to take in *throw-aways*, a term for children who are not runaways by choice, but who are discarded by the adults in their lives. When a child enters one of these safe havens, parents would be encouraged to

158

schedule visits with their children to try to repair the family unit.

Parents who are unwilling to keep appointments, thus showing a disinterest in their child's well-being, would not be given custody of their children until they demonstrated more responsible behavior.

All social security funds, SSI, ADC, food stamps, and child support payments would follow the child into the group home. Working parents would be charged for their child's expenses on a sliding scale basis.

Critics might say that some young people would use this safe haven as a refuge from acceptable but strict parental rules; however, the safe havens would also have strict rules to follow to give children the structure they need in their lives.

When many people think of group homes, they envision a draconian picture of cold, damp institutions ran by a heartless staff. My experience indicates this Dickensian stereotype is not true. I have talked with hundreds of children who have stayed or are currently living in group homes and shelters. They have all reported humane treatment, and many are happier and more content than they have ever been in their lives.

* * * * *

Todd invited me to dinner at his Children's Home. The meal was wonderful. I asked him if the food was always this good. He said, "No. It's always good, but you're being served a 'Sunday-company's-coming-to-dinner' meal."

I told him that this was just how I lived: Company's dinners were always more elaborate than busy weekday meals.

* * * * *

I asked Beth how she was doing at the Guardian Center. She said she was fine; her sister was in the wing with the babies, but she still got to see her a lot.

Everybody had to go to bed at nine o'clock, but she didn't mind because she was sleeping real well.

* * * * *

Michelle liked her group home. She told me they were going to be taken shopping at the mall on Saturday. Everybody was going to go bowling on Sunday.

Michelle was doing better than she had ever done before in school, and she seemed much happier than when she lived at home.

* * * * *

Amy lived with her mother, a serious crack addict, and her grandmother. When her grandmother got sick, Amy was taken into the Guardian Center. When her grandmother died, one of the ladies who worked there took Amy to the funeral. Amy told me that it was this lady's day off, but she gave up her free time to take her.

Amy was awed that someone had cared enough about her to do this.

Amy will be living in this shelter for years. It is wonderful that the people there show such care and devotion to their young charges.

* * * * *

We will have fewer children on the streets, abused or neglected at home, and growing into unloving or uncaring adults if we can make sure that every child who needs a safe haven--whether for a few days or a few years--has one available.

The cycle of neglect, abuse, and despair can be broken if we care enough about our children in need to give them safe havens.

SCHOLARSHIPS

If we want to encourage people to do their best, then we need to reward those who excel. Unfortunately, nowadays this policy is the exception rather than the rule.

Today the term *scholarship* is a misnomer because awards are extensively given primarily on the basis of need, rather than scholastic abilities. Many low performing students have free rides as well as individual tutoring, mentoring, and special classes to try to make them successful in college-- while many high performing students get little or no scholarship money at all.

Superficially, this policy may sound fair; however, it leads to quite a lot of problems:

- Students don't study as hard because good grades and high test scores are not rewarded by this practice.

- Families may appear to have greater need than they do because of inaccurate or misleading information. More often, families which seem to be able to pay for their child's education may not actually be able to do so without great sacrifice.

And some parents selfishly choose not to do so, and thus their child does without.

- This practice does not promote having the best possible qualified people being prepared for our country's future. The resulting fallout could adversely impact the quality of future teachers, engineers, nurses, and doctors, among many others. Don't we owe it to future generations to give aid to the best and the brightest?

We need to consider giving scholarships based on grades, test scores, papers, and portfolios. By so doing, each student may earn a scholarship regardless of his or her family's commitment to education. Most people have no problem giving athletic scholarships based on ability: Why not do academics the same way? Is not the quality of future professionals in this country more important than ball games?

Poor children would be able to earn their scholarships based on ability, just like everyone else. Presently, urban and poor children face the discrimination of being considered not as capable as their suburban peers. The idea that children from poorer families are intrinsically less competent, and so can't compete equally if expected to is insulting.

If there is not enough money to go around, it is only sensible for a community to choose those who are best academically prepared in order to enrich the community as a whole. This approach would not close the door to higher education for the others. They could take classes part-time while they work and reapply for scholarships based on new grades; save up money while working full time; seek employment in companies with educational assistance; join the military or National Guard; borrow money (educational debt is no worse than car debt, which most young people willingly assume); ask for tuition money as holiday gifts from family members; work during high school summers; or work part-time during high school years.

The policy of parceling out money based on ability rewards the best and hardest-working students, and motivates younger classmates to try harder. It would also help slow down the painful, expensive process of flunking out the ill-prepared. Not only are people not owed an education; you can't give one away to someone who isn't interested.

ALTERNATIVE SCHOOLS

Alternative schools for students with behavior problems exist in many large school districts today. They may or may not include special education students; they may only be for students expelled from regular school; they might not be available to those already expelled; they may be a mandated program; or enrollment might be by parental choice. Whatever the designated population, alternative schools are quite expensive due to very low pupil-teacher ratios, extra staff and security, and additional transportation and building costs, all of which use educational funds which would otherwise be spent on improving regular class instruction.

While many public officials tout alternative schools as a way to get "trouble-makers" out of regular schools, the actual success of the alternative schools is getting less attention than is deserved in view of the expenditure of time and money involved. Unfortunately, many alternative programs have been developed under the premises that increasing student self-esteem and providing unconditional positive regard will result in improved behavior and increased learning without sufficient evidence to support these assumptions.

My personal experience shows alternative schools are places where hard-working, stressed-out teachers try to teach uncaring students.

* * * * *

A young man sat talking with me about returning to regular school while fiddling under the table. When I asked him to please place his hands on top of the desk, I found a home-made knife he had been sharpening to a razor point. When I took it from him and told him he could have no such item in a high school, he stated he wouldn't return to school without "protection," and preferred to remain in the alternative school.

* * * * *

At a different alternative school a group of young men being considered for return to regular high school sat around a table, each vying to tell more elaborate stories of misbehavior. No one seemed too anxious to return to the normal school setting.

Basic behavior and moral development were still low, nor had their educational skill levels improved.

* * * * *

To be effective, alternative schools need to be controlled, regimented classrooms emphasizing basic skills. They should be made just unpleasant enough by lack of such amenities as field trips, pizza parties, and opportunities for socializing that students want to return to the regular school population.

Assignment to alternative schools should be for one or two semesters at the most. If six to ten months of instruction do not modify a student's behavior, then this approach probably is not the best placement for him.

The value of any alternative school should be judged on its capability to help students fit back into regular school by meeting minimum social behavior standards. This research would be easy to do. After a year in the alternative program, students would be returned to regular school. Records of their discipline problems, attendance, and grades could be compared to the same before they entered the alternative program.

Perhaps results could be compared against a control group of behavior problem students who did not go to the alternative school. While some maturing of students may skew results, overall success or failure of the program would be very clear. Any adjustments in program strategies could be made and successful programs could be cloned without wasting more precious educational dollars.

PUBLIC AND PRIVATE SCHOOL ACHIEVEMENT

Private schools tend to have higher achieving and better-behaved students because they get to pick their students. Even a private school located in an urban area that enrolls students from impoverished homes still gets a different population than the local public school. These differences come about because of the following reasons:

- Parents of private school children show they are committed to education by attending interviews and pre-school meetings. Public schools help students whose parents may not be at all interested in their children. For example, many evening open houses in urban schools are very sparsely attended.

- The majority of private schools are selective when they enroll special needs students. They tend to take only those with the most promise of success in keeping up with their peers. Public schools educate all students from the very gifted to children who haven't enough brain function to focus their eyes--and all levels and types in between.

- Private schools can and do ask nonproductive students to leave. I have enrolled a number of private school students with *circled grades* on their report cards--passing grades to take with them to the public schools but grades that would turn into *"F's"* if the parent tried to keep the child in the private school. Tricks such as this, which are used to encourage poorer performing students to leave the private school, increase the highly publicized achievement rates of private schools.

- When private school students misbehave to the point of detracting from their own or others' instructional time, they are simply asked to leave. I have enrolled private school students in the middle of school semesters because parents were told to take their child out of private schooling, and into public schools, without even a twenty-four hour notice. Needless to say, these students' lack of effort and misbehaviors take public school teacher time away from teaching and focuses it on discipline--which leads to lower achievement test scores. In the meantime, private school scores are likely to improve after weeding out such students.

- When young people are released from juvenile detention, boot camp programs, troubled youth homes, and drug and alcohol centers, they enroll in public, not private schools. These students coming into classrooms at all times of the year also reflect negatively on public school test scores.

- The transfer rate of students is much higher for public than private schools. It is not uncommon for some urban youths to move more than five times a year. This means a teacher is much less likely to have a student for a full school year. He cannot teach the child who isn't there, and frequent moves greatly impede academic growth.

We need to stop pitting private and public schools against each other; and we need to quit heaping accolades on the former and criticism on the latter. They both perform a valuable service in educating our youth while serving very different populations.

SUPERINTENDENTS AND SCHOOL BOARDS

Revolving door superintendents are the norm in large school districts. Most school heads stay in their jobs less than five years; then they move on to greener pastures or are let go by their school boards.

If we can't have superintendents who work their way up the ladder--as a teacher, counselor, dean, principal, superintendent--then we need superintendents who at least stay put long enough to see the results of their programs. What we tend to get now is mostly flash, glitter, and hype.

In job interviews the outside applicant dazzles the interview committee with innovative ideas and promises to turn everything around until all students are achieving above grade level and all parents are happy and content. When hired, the superintendent's first year in a large system is mainly used getting to know the facilities, staff, and community. Then come the changes--usually of a large scale in order to stimulate news journalists into giving the superintendent extensive press coverage. Good preparation will not be done because speed of implementation is more important for the superintendents' and school board members' resumes than is accuracy.

When problems occur--and problems always occur with massive undertakings--the board blames the superintendent and becomes disillusioned; thus a negative relationship begins.

Board/Superintendent relationships tend to be manic depressive, with euphoric highs and extreme lows due to unrealistic expectation levels. Before the change cycle can be completed, a new superintendent is hired who scraps the old plan, spends a year just getting to know his way around town, implements his vision with too little planning, and the cycle continues--with the students and teachers paying the tab in terms of lack of follow-through, instability, and a tremendous waste of taxpayer dollars.

We need superintendents who are willing to commit to their communities. They need to face the outcome of their policies when they go to the grocery store, church, or gasoline station. They need to stay put long enough to care about the people and feel like they are home. School boards should not seek out superintendents who hop from job to job for a few extra thousands--like free agents in sports--moving toward the highest bidder. School boards need to hire personnel who they feel reflect the values and direction of the community, and then the board needs to stay committed over the long haul, rough patches and all.

School boards may need to review their own roles in education and emphasize macro-management instead of micro-management. Term limits, elected teacher representation, and elected business leaders sitting on the boards are all areas which need to be discussed. Election to boards of education should not be used as political stepping stones nor as opportunities for recognition, power, or revenge, but as a sincere way to improve the lot of all of our children.

TEACHER EXCHANGE

Urban teachers are taking a hard rap for the perceived failures of inner city schools: lack of discipline, low standardized test scores, high school drop-out rates, and below grade level skills in math and reading. Critics insist that the problem lies with ill-prepared, uncaring and lazy urban teachers whose unions demand large salaries for little work.

If the root cause of public city schools' woes is simply inferior teachers, this is good news because the problem could be easily remedied with a teacher exchange program.

Through the years there have been many foreign teacher exchange programs, with each teacher taking the other's place in their native country. The rationale behind these swaps is for each teacher to learn from his new environment and to share knowledge with temporary colleagues, thereby enriching the staff and students at both schools.

A localized exchange program could help improve our public schools. Within an eighty mile radius both "good" suburban and "bad" urban schools can usually be found. A local exchange

176

could be set up with the expert teachers from high-achieving schools trading places with teachers from problematic schools.

The teachers going to the better schools would learn new teaching methods from their new surroundings to take back with them when they return to their old schools. The teachers from suburbia coming into the low-achieving, poorly disciplined schools could be role models for all the teachers in the inner city school.

I know that urban teachers would be clamoring to take advantage of this growth opportunity. I can only hope that suburban teachers would be equally willing to share their expertise in the urban setting.

TEACHER PAY

American teachers traditionally have come primarily from two sources:

- Rather poor but bookish first-generation college-educated people. School teaching for these people was seen as a first step in upward mobility, and away from working class labor.

- Intelligent women when few other choices in life--nurse, teacher, or secretary--were being offered. Of course, this situation has changed.

Now schools must compete with nearly unlimited employment opportunities for bright, caring people of all races, gender, and backgrounds. When college-bound students consider the beginning pay of teachers, the low status of teachers, and the stresses and frustrations of teaching, public school jobs are not the typical first career choice for the best and the brightest.

What needs to be done to attract higher-quality individuals into teaching?

The initial low teaching salaries need to be made more compatible to other college majors.

Most public schools use a pay scale which increases with each year of experience and with increased education. Thus, a school with four third-grade teachers teaching the same hours and doing the same work might be paying the teachers $19,800, $24,000, $47,300, and $50,200.

The teachers at the top of the scale can live a middle-class (but not lavish) life style, but many newer teachers' children can qualify for reduced meals and textbooks, since their college-graduate parents' pay is so low.

We need to raise the beginning pay of teachers in order to make the profession more attractive to talented people. This change may require phasing out the multi-tiered pay scales now used. Starting salaries would be higher, and the difference between the highest and lowest pay for the same job would be much narrower.

Most experienced teachers would fight this change with the outcry that they have worked all the lowly-paid years to finally obtain the higher pay. To lose it now would cut their lifetime earnings and eventual retirement benefits. For this reason, pay changes would be put into place much like the federal government changed its retirement program several years ago. No change would occur for those already hired, but new hires would be under the new system. Current teachers should recognize the need for schools to be financially competitive in getting the most capable people to teach our children.

While the overwhelming majority of America's teachers are hard-working, dedicated, competent people, the current system of multi-tiered pay encourages the less competent to stay too long. The idea of finally making a reasonable salary after years of teaching has some teachers staying on the job because they need to "financially average out" their teaching careers (to make up for lost early income), rather than to enter a new field of endeavor. Extra pay for additional education and extra duties, a modest four or five-tiered pay system for experience, and cost of living increases would serve most school systems best.

SPECIAL EDUCATION

Special education has also changed the face of the public school system. Rather than being left at home or shuttled off to special schools, children with all types of handicaps now are served in regular public schools.

This trend is quite a change from when special needs students were educated entirely in special education classes and special schools. Twenty-two years ago I was a teacher who integrated physically-handicapped students into a regular high school, after the closing of a self-contained building where physically-handicapped students had been bused. This experience was very rewarding.

The students' handicaps ranged from a short left leg that simply needed a built-up shoe to a young man without arms and legs. All of the students were successfully integrated into a regular high school with some assistance and use of special devices.

My learning-disabled and emotionally-handicapped students also became part of the school as a whole and were helped by being in the regular school surroundings.

Currently, students with the most severely handicapping conditions are enrolled into regular schools. Young bodies who are incapable of registering their surroundings at all due to extremely low intellectual functioning are rolled into school buildings.

* * * * *

One heart-breaking fourteen-year-old girl lay on a mat each day in a regular high school and cried.

She was unable to communicate or interact with others; she couldn't walk or even crawl, and did not even grasp for objects as most infants do. She was tended to exactly like a three-month old baby: Diapers were changed and she had to be fed.

Although communication with her was difficult, she seemed unhappy when moved around or jostled by other students.

* * * * *

A seventeen-year-old who was proud to be toilet trained started undressing herself in the high school hallway on her way to the restroom.

She was oblivious of the other regular teenage students around her.

* * * * *

Fourteen-year-old Molly wore crutches and braces when she enrolled in a regular school. Another teacher and I took a bus-load of students to a city park for a field trip and picnic.

Molly was able to swing for the first time in her life that day with just a little bit of help. She was thrilled as we pushed her higher and higher.

Molly hiked so much that day that she needed new rubber caps for her crutches because she had worn them out having fun.

* * * * *

David, an emotionally disturbed youngster, was sitting inside a large cardboard box, placed inside a small closet in a little-used hallway in the school.

It took three months for David to become a part of the regular school. First I had to convince him to give up the safety of his cardboard box, and then I got him to move out of a hidden hall closet

183

into a classroom closet where I placed a school desk for him.

David then allowed the door of the closet to be left open so he could see other students, and they could see him.

After months, David joined the class and had a friend.

* * * * *

Richard, a thirteen-year-old, had never attended school before. For several weeks he did not interact with other students.

One day a breakthrough occurred when Billy started talking to him and teasing him.

Richard, who had no arms or legs, used the ability he did have and bit Billy.

While I had to discipline Richard for biting, which is never appropriate in school, this did show that Richard was beginning to come out of his shell.

* * * * *

Calvin, a thirteen-year-old learning-disabled student, said with total satisfaction after a *week of one-on-one instruction using colored building blocks, "Wow, I never thought I would learn to multiply!".*

* * * * *

When comparing public schools, past and present, or with private schools, the tremendous cost of special education must be considered. Helping special populations costs much money in equipment, supplies, and additional personnel; and it costs time for additional planning, behavior management, and case conferencing. (A case conference is a meeting during which parents, regular and special educators, a psychologist, administrators, and others determine special needs for children with educational handicaps.)

Also, burdensome federal compliance requirements take up much valuable teacher time and take some of the best special education teachers out of the classroom altogether to do governmental paper work. Large school corporations now spend millions of dollars each year on multi-layers of bureaucracy just to meet federal requirements.

The special needs population of a school must also be accounted for when judging the success of a school's graduates. It is very possible that when a future employer complains of a high school graduate "who can't read past third-grade level," he is referring to a special education student who has reached a high level (for him) of reading, and has become integrated into normal society only through the efforts of a number of public school teachers. Fifty years ago this same youth might have stayed at home, never learning any academic skills at all.

Please note that in most places legal requirements forbid the mention of special education or any other program which indicates ability level on high school diplomas.

As wonderful as the opportunity to attend regular schools and learn and grow to the fullest potential has been for many special students, the amount of time and money being directed away from the general school population, and towards the special needs population, may have gone too far in some cases.

A trend which has developed in the last twenty years has been for schools to provide very costly special services which do not directly relate to academic functioning for handicapped students. For example, schools now routinely are expected to provide physical therapy and occupational therapy within the school and to do so for years beyond the usual time limits prescribed in hospitals. Physical and occupational therapy should be taken out of the schools and returned to the hospitals.

Parents of special education students have also demanded reflexology, dance therapy, massage therapy, myotherapy, swim therapy, horseback riding, home computer systems, and individual lap tops. The concept behind these demands is that schools (and taxpayers) must provide any and all items, services, lessons, or equipment which the parent and case conference committee think might be beneficial to the child. In their quest to find solutions to their child's problems, parents can become quite unreasonable, and often are unaware that giving too much to special children often denies goods and services for non-special education students.

Therefore, we suggest that special needs students be provided with the same educational opportunities as the general student population. However, they should not be provided with expensive special services which do not directly relate to increased academic functioning.

Neither should special needs students receive special services which are not provided to the regular school population. For example, if horseback riding is not offered to regular students, neither should it be available for children in special programs. But even with these limitations, special education is going to entail extra costs for public schools which swell far beyond private school expenditures.

Many fear that special education costs are crushing regular education. Although special education is very important, we need to guard against over-zealously advocated special programs which relate only marginally to attainment of traditional academic skills.

BEAUTIFUL SURROUNDINGS

Our physical environment plays an important role in our moods, attitudes, and behaviors. In view of this fact, it is unfortunate that many older schools tend to be dingy, damaged places, and even many newer buildings are drab and dull. Situations such as these are in sharp contrast to some public schools in wealthy areas: In one case the state had to halt a luxurious school plan which included such opulence as private Jacuzzis and marble, gilded restrooms.

As a general rule, students from less affluent homes must go to less attractive schools. The message to students is clear: *You aren't used to much, you aren't worth much, and therefore we (the community) won't bother to provide you much.*

Teachers sitting at World War II surplus desks looking at pealing-paint walls wonder about the priorities of the community. How much worse for the child to have to go home to an even uglier place! Schools should be havens of culture and beauty in otherwise depressing, discouraged lives.

So what needs to be done? Basic cleanliness could be improved at no cost by using student and teacher labor, while custodial staff would still do large and possibly dangerous jobs. Students could particularly benefit from this change by learning to be more responsible.

Unfortunately, students no longer clean chalk boards and erasers in most schools, but under the new plan they could do these things and much more. Younger children could care for their own classrooms, sweep halls, dust, and wash sinks. Older students could have designated school time for school cleaning, perhaps two hours a week. The entire student body should become involved in maintaining and beautifying their own environment.

Several things would be accomplished in addition to a nicer looking school: Students would learn how to take care of their surroundings and learn basic cleaning and maintenance skills. They would feel some ownership regarding what happens to school property, and most importantly, they would learn that everyone must do this kind of labor, the concept being if you use it, you can clean it.

Nowadays too many students think they are too good for menial labor and that others exist to clean up their messes. When schools have tried to assign custodial work as punishment, parents have protested that their child will not do embarrassing, demeaning work. This concept, however, does not view maintenance work as demeaning, or as punishment, but as a necessary part of everyone's life.

Culture and beauty could be added rather cheaply, too. Sponge-painted walls in non-institutional colors, old-fashioned tan roller shades softened with stencils, appropriate bibelots, and nonvocal music in halls and lunchrooms could all improve the atmosphere a great deal.

I always have fresh flowers in my room (thanks to a doting husband). Students rarely fail to comment on them, asking what kind of flowers they are and what the colors are called. Even young criminals court ordered to school have discussed my flowers and reproduction prints on the wall.

Although I have had several adults tell me I shouldn't have nice things at school, none of these things have been stolen or vandalized. However, the same cannot be said about my credit cards and money, so I am not promoting foolhardiness in the classroom. By the way, be careful of driving a red car to school: The red seems to flash "steal me."

More expensive luxuries, like carpet and air conditioning, can be added whenever possible. I found it ironic and sad that a nation-wide fast food outlet (not McDonalds), near a school in a neighborhood of blighted, chopped-up apartment homes, did not have air conditioning during very hot weather. I have never noticed such lack of basic comforts in similar outlets in up-scale areas, where purchasers can take their food to comfortable homes; but in a dreary area during sweltering heat the same amount of money spent for a hamburger and cola did not provide a little air-conditioned relief.

Some people go from lovely homes to climate-controlled cars to jobs and schools with all creature comforts provided in restaurants and stores which cater to their needs; others have no place or space that ever lifts their spirits or gives them physical comfort. Our youth see this dual treatment and recognize the lack of value placed on them. Shouldn't our local, state, and federal governments try to be more even-handed in providing adequate learning facilities?

A pitiful joke told to students and staff in one school plagued by a 94° temperature and dozens of daily bee stings questioned why the school couldn't at least move into the nineteenth century and have window screens. (We knew better than to expect air conditioners. Teachers had offered to buy window units with their own money but were denied the right to do this because of costs due to the additional electricity and rules requiring union installations.)

It's easy to understand a lack of student motivation in a basement level, stinking-hot classroom with the smell and noise of big-wheeled trucks coming from the stone-crushing center down the street, only two and a half feet from the classroom window.

BUSINESSES HELPING SCHOOLS

Many business leaders have expressed concern over the problems the public schools are facing and have even offered their assistance in helping students and teachers.

One of the most positive business involvements with schools I have seen came from businesses opening their doors to students to visit. Field trips are not just a day trip away from the classroom but allow youngsters to experience a new piece of the world first hand. Many adults can still recall school field trips from years ago as highlights of their growing up years.

* * * * *

Navistar, which manufactures large engines, opened its doors to a class of mine one year. We walked by huge, burning fires, passed workers assemblying units, saw robotics technology at work, and were served free lunches (thanks to Navistar) in the plant cafeteria.

My students were awed. One boy asked me if I had ever seen anything so exciting, how they started with just a block of raw material and ended up with a truck engine. He had had no idea how such things were made. Judging by the excitement of his voice and his smiling face, I'm sure he'll always remember this visit.

Another boy at Navistar stood watching one man working at a machine for more than ten minutes. Afterwards he came to me and said "I could learn how to do that! I could get a job at a place like this!" This fatherless, welfare, inner-city young man had seen himself as capable of entering the middle-class work place in the future for the first time.

The head of the Navistar plant graciously gave his time to answer student questions about requirements of various jobs, employment of minorities and women, pay scales, and work expectations.

By allowing a busload of school children to get a real view of a working environment, a caring company may have changed a few lives for the better and given an interesting memory to many.

* * * * *

It would be nice if more companies could arrange field trips--nothing fancy or special planned, just a real look at a paper factory, food processing plant, behind the scenes at a restaurant or hotel, or even a stroll through the huge offices of insurance companies or other businesses where real people work to support themselves and their families.

I even took a high school class on a field trip to a mortuary. From learning about different kinds of caskets to finding out where the blood goes during embalming, this too was an interesting learning experience for all.

Ideally, every student would be able to take two field trips each school year. The only thing stopping most children from having these experiences is the lack of invitations from businesses and the cost of bus transportation from poorer school systems.

A second extremely meaningful experience provided to my students by various business leaders was an opportunity for some of them to have a formal dining experience.

* * * * *

I drove several small groups of students to professional sports luncheons at a Hyatt hotel; additional seats for inner-city students were paid for by community business leaders.

The young men were just as interested as the girls in learning correct table manners and behaviors. They questioned me about what to expect and how to act. Afterwards, they initiated a review session so they would be more comfortable the next time.

The students said they had never eaten a meal in a restaurant with a white table cloth, silver flatware, and goblets. While not always completely sure of what they were eating, they did eat everything and enjoyed themselves immensely.

* * * * *

I took Yolanda to another free-ticket luncheon, an experience so wonderful for her I doubt that the business sponsor could even begin to imagine what happiness he gave her.

I had previously worked with several members of Yolanda's family; her mother was a drug-dealing, cocaine-using prostitute who first came to my attention shortly after Christmas, when an older sister reported that she had neglected and abused them.

On Christmas Eve one of the mother's boyfriends said she ought to buy her kids something for Christmas (she didn't routinely buy gifts or clothing for her children), and he gave her some money. The mother went to the liquor store and bought each child ages six to fifteen her very own six-pack of wine cooler for Christmas morning. Unfortunately, this made the younger child ill.

Yolanda had never been in a restaurant with a menu. She was nervous and unbelievably excited, had taken great care with her hair and appearance that day, and needed lots of reassurance that her clothing would be acceptable. When we walked into the Hyatt dining area, she gasped, "I've seen things like this before on television!"

When she cut her broccoli spear it slid across the plate and onto the table. She almost panicked, but a nice waiter came to her aid by sweeping the cloth clean and offering her more broccoli. He also served her two desserts--both chocolate mousse, another new experience!

Yolanda left that lunch happier and prouder than I have ever seen her: She had conquered a new challenge.

* * * * *

If business leaders could provide more poverty-level youths with an opportunity to practice social skills and become comfortable in "formal" settings such as these, it would help them enter the mainstream of working America.

A third way the business community could help public schools is by using the schools' services. While some suburban schools are able to raise needed money by selling candy, having chili dinners, and other fund-raising activities, poorer schools often have families who cannot afford to even join the parent teacher organization.

Businesses could support the public schools located near them. If a holiday luncheon is needed, why not ask a nearby high school if they could prepare it in foods class? Students could wait tables, and the music department might even provide choral selections of your choice.

In addition, art departments could design simple in-house materials for various purposes. Industrial technology departments might also be able to help businesses with some of their projects. The money paid for these things would help provide new materials for the classroom.

Need to rent a gym, classroom, or auditorium during evenings or weekends? The local high school might be able to help for a small donation.

199

Come to our plays and programs. They might not be as good as a Broadway production, but the tickets will be much cheaper and the cast will be even more grateful than seasoned professionals to see groups of business men and women at these often meagerly-attended events.

Let us sell you candy bars for band uniforms, greeting cards for new computers, and plush toys for library books by putting order forms from the local schools into your place of business. Or donate the profits from one vending machine in the break room to a neighborhood school.

Public schools need your money, but not just as a handout or charity. Students would take great pride and satisfaction from earning their way with your help.

BUSINESS MODELS
IN THE SCHOOLS

Prevailing hot business trends such as quality circles, total quality management, customer-driven service, etc., often filter down into use in the school systems after a couple of years' delay. These may not always be helpful since teaching is a much more complex, personality-centered endeavor than most businesses.

Many business journals have published articles on public school woes using the business/customer motif. They have suggested that schools should be viewed the same as private industry, which must please their customers or go out of business. This might be a useful approach except that proponents invariably get the relationships wrong: They say the student is the schools' customer, and that teachers must cater to their needs.

Our students are not our customers; therefore, we should not arrange school in such a way that the student customer "buys" our services. Students are the product, parents are the suppliers of the materials, the schools are the processors, and the community at large is the customer.

Public Schools exist because all taxpayers have a stake in the final product. Therefore, schools must please a unified community by producing sound, knowledgeable, moral citizens, rather than pleasing students by catering to their whims.

Parents supply the raw material, children. This statement has two implications:

- If schools don't process the students well, parents will send their raw materials elsewhere.

- All material doesn't start the same, and so must be processed differently to result in equally good but different end products. You can't make a cherry high-boy out of oak, or a sturdy oak book case from ash, but fine workable furniture can be made from all the lumber with the help of skilled, caring craftsmen.

We needn't belabor the translation of business acumen into school vernacular. However, everyone in America these days is a self-proclaimed expert in education. While teachers and schools have much to gain from ideas from well-meaning leaders in the business community and other backgrounds, our children's educations are too important to be driven by fads or poorly-fitting conceptual models.

It is time for teachers to re-assume a leadership role in the field of education. Many or most experienced teachers know exactly what is needed to improve our schools, and yet their cries go unheeded in favor of many outsiders who don't have a clue regarding what teachers must face each day.

EMPLOYMENT FOR STUDENTS

The best way businesses can help young people enter the world of work is to actually open their doors wide for them to enter. Businesses need to hire young people for true, real-life employment with much the same expectations they have for all workers. This is not to suggest that busy work should be developed for them; youths need to see that they are giving real service for real wages.

Well-intended youth jobs programs, where youngsters are hired to sit around because no real work is needed, don't help beyond giving them a little spending money. These made-up, often government-sponsored jobs do not fool the participants, who laugh and joke about getting their money for sitting around talking or watching movies or TV. These jobs are worse than just a waste of taxpayer dollars. They teach young people to be irresponsible workers, which is just the opposite of their well-intended purpose.

Give youths real work at decent wages for them to develop positive work skills. These are the jobs students talk about with pride of accomplishment. They want to bus tables, wash cars, file records, sort laundry, do landscaping and phone solicitation, work fast food, paint, and help the elderly to earn money.

A particularly necessary but harsh job in the Midwest is corn detasseling. Every fall I have inner-city students who tell me about being taken in busloads during the summer to farm fields to walk up and down, row after row, of planted corn in the hot, humid sun, detasseling as they go along. They talk about singing and music on the bus, cookouts in the fields, humane treatment, making friends, and earning good wages. The pride in their voices and smiles on their faces show they recognize their own accomplishments. On the other hand, those with made-up jobs seldom show such pride in their accomplishments.

Along with hiring students for real work, businesses must also be willing to fire them for unsatisfactory performance if the students are to grow into productive members of society.

* * * * *

La Tasha, who had a part-time job at a fast food restaurant, was furious because she'd been fired from her job due to a "trick."

A badly dressed black man had come up to her counter and was slow in deciding what to order.

She told him "Make up your f--king mind. I'm not standing here all day for you!"

He took her to the back office and fired her. She felt tricked because he was poorly dressed, didn't act right, and was a black man. La Tasha, a black student, said she didn't know a black man would be the owner of several fast food establishments.

We talked for awhile about this learning experience and how she would take her improved knowledge base to her next job.

* * * * *

Another way the business community can help people become working contributors to our society is to hire people who have learned from negative job experiences; being fired should not eliminate young people from the job pool. Many people, but particularly youths, learn from being fired and do better the next time.

In summary, employers can help young people become productive workers by

- hiring them for necessary, meaningful work for decent wages;

- having high expectations for behavior; (Don't be afraid to correct them, chastise them, or even fire those who don't measure up.)

- rehiring people who have learned from negative work experiences and are willing to improve.

If employers are concerned that hiring fourteen, fifteen, and sixteen-year-olds would compromise school achievement by taking away study time, a modest study done by the authors in 1995 showed that grades tended to be higher for students who worked eight to twenty hours a week during the school year. Overwhelmingly, the failing students did not have jobs, and so were neither gaining job skills nor a general education. They reported spending their time sleeping, watching cable, and "hanging around."

Getting into the true job market and gaining real-life work experience during the teen years would only enhance most students' development by teaching them pride in accomplishment and responsible work habits.

DUMMYING DOWN

Schools at all levels are part of the trend toward lowered expectations. A Big Ten college administrator described the proliferation of remedial and lighter classes at his university as "a response to the reality of students today." However, in this chicken-and-egg cycle, this university is in fact helping develop the remedial reality in which the administrator works. Since high schoolers know the college of their choice will not require them to have studied difficult material, many naturally don't bother to do so, causing the colleges to close the loop in the self-fulfilling prophecy.

The message sent to students is *give as little effort as you like, and someone else will make it okay later.*

As long as universities continue to accept less-than-adequately prepared students to offset decreasing enrollments, students will not listen to guidance counselors telling them to take challenging courses.

INDIVIDUAL DIFFERENCES

We often hear people say that students shouldn't be promoted until they perform up to their grade placement. Is this practice feasible or even possible? Before this question can be answered, let us first consider what psychologists and educators have discovered about individual differences in academic achievement.

For many years psychologists and educators have known that individual differences in academic abilities exist for individuals in our population and that such differences can be plotted into a bell-shaped curve such as this:

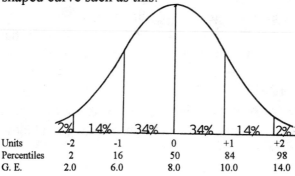

	2%	14%	34%	34%	14%	2%

Units	-2	-1	0	+1	+2
Percentiles	2	16	50	84	98
G. E.	2.0	6.0	8.0	10.0	14.0

Notes

1. "Units" are actually standard deviation units.

2. G. E. is Grade Equivalents.

3. All percentages are fairly close approximations to exact figures for the normal curve.

4. Most depictions of the normal curve show three or more units above and below the average. Only two units are shown here for the sake of simplicity.

5. Actual grade equivalent scores under the normal curve will vary according to which test is used. However, different normal curve units and percentiles should be similar to these for most standardized tests.

209

Note that the right half of the curve is a mirror image of the left; the majority of scores on a test, say in reading, would be within the large hump near the center; the highest scores would be to the extreme right; and lowest scores would be to the extreme left. This curve, often called the normal curve, is divided into what we shall call normal curve units counted off as plus and minus one and two above and below the average, which is in the center.

We know from experience that these units, which are calculated by a mathematical procedure, usually contain the percentages of the population which are indicated in each segment of the curve: Note that half, or 50 per cent of the scores are above, and half are below, the average score. The majority of the scores--about 68 per cent--fall in the middle where the hump is biggest, from +1 to -1 units from the average. Approximately 14 per cent fall between +1 and +2, and from -1 to -2 units above and below the average. Only about 2 per cent of the scores fall two or more units above and below the average.

Let us examine the reading grade equivalent scores from a standardized achievement test for a group of beginning eighth graders. If the students were randomly selected from throughout the U.S., the results would probably be similar to the normal curve.

Many of the eighth graders should earn scores fairly close to the average or 50th percentile score of 8.0. However, because of individual differences, some will score above and below this average. About 34 per cent would score from the 8th to the 10th grade equivalents, and approximately 34 per cent would earn 6th to 8th grade equivalents (see grade equivalents under the normal curve.)

You can see where this is going. About 14 per cent would score from the 10th to the 14th grade equivalents, and the same percentage would score from the 2nd to the 6th grade on the test. Only about 2 per cent will score above, and 2 per cent below, the 14th and 2nd grade equivalents.

When applied to a class of 30 beginning eighth graders in a school system with a diverse population, the distribution of scores probably would be close to the following:

10 would fall between the 16th and 50th percentiles.
10 would fall between the 50th and 84th percentiles.
4 would fall between the 84th and 98th percentiles.

4 would fall between the 2nd and 16th percentiles.

1 would fall above the 98th percentile.

1 would fall below the 2nd percentile.

These numbers come from multiplying the percentage of cases in each segment of the normal curve times 30 students.

Although individual differences were illustrated using reading scores on a standardized test, similar differences exist for students in most other academic areas. Furthermore, although our example concerns grade equivalent scores, similar differences should apply to actual grade level functioning in the classroom.

By now it should be obvious that it is unrealistic to expect all students to perform academically up to grade level. We should no more expect all children to read on grade level than we should expect all people to be six feet tall, to have brown eyes, or to run the mile in less than four minutes.

It is strange that many of the same people who accept individual differences in athletic abilities wish to impose an arbitrary, unattainable academic standard on our children. It is also interesting how many people accept individual differences at the upper--but not the lower--end of the normal curve. For example, many of the same people who expect some students to perform above grade level believe all the other students should be able to function on grade level, thus ignoring the lower end of the normal curve.

So in view of individual differences, should we give up trying to get our children up to grade level academically? Quite the contrary, we should use all available means to help each child achieve as high on the curve that he or she is capable of doing. In the meantime, however, we should not be surprised if, even with the best possible teaching, some students will fall short of this mark.

And we should also guard against the establishment of policies (i.e., all must read on grade level to be promoted) in the public schools which fail to take into account the broad range of individual differences in our children. This warning is particularly directed at schools which serve a broad range of children from various diverse backgrounds.

Promoting low-functioning students to higher grades often is done for practical considerations, which relate to social and sexual development. For example, would you really want your fourth grade daughter to sit next to a fifteen-year-old boy who is almost six feet tall? Would this be fair to the fifteen-year-old, who needs socialization with peers of similar age? This kind of scenario would be a frequent occurrence if slow students were not promoted to keep them with students of somewhat similar age and development.

So now we know that children throughout the U.S. will vary tremendously in academic capabilities. But what factors seem to influence where they fall on the normal curve?

Note that I did not ask which factors cause some students to achieve higher than others because, in general, evidence of cause-effect relationships in this area is not available. (However, we do know that some factors which negatively impact on normal development, such as severe nutritional deficits and damage to the central nervous system, can make achievement up to grade level very difficult.)

Nevertheless, a number of factors have been identified which are related to academic functioning. Some of them are the following:

educational levels of parents
occupational levels of parents
family income
IQ's of parents
IQ of student
the quality of stimulation in the home

214

family values (are reading materials made available to the children; is education truly valued, etc.?)

achievement motivation of student
emotional stability of student
genetic predispositions for learning.

In general, higher ratings on those factors in this list which can be rated--such as income, educational, and occupational levels of parents and IQ's--generally are related to higher student academic achievement. On the other hand, lower ratings in these areas are often related to relatively lower academic achievement.

However, there are many exceptions to this general trend. Some students from families with higher income, education, IQ's, etc., fail to achieve within the upper half of the curve, while others from impoverished backgrounds perform at the higher end of the curve.

For many years it has been known that students in private schools as a group usually score higher on achievement tests than their public school counterparts. Why might this be?

The reason is simple. Because admission requirements based on criteria such as previous grades, high achievement test scores, and hefty tuition and transportation costs required for many private schools selectively eliminate most students from low income backgrounds, with poorly educated parents, who make lower grades and score lower on achievement tests.

Teachers in private schools usually do not have to tolerate extreme behavior-problem students because these children are sent back to the public schools. (Students returned to public schools often say they were frequently threatened to be "kicked out" of their private schools if behavior problems continued.)

In other words, to a large extent private schools are instructing students from the upper end of the normal curve--or at least excluding many from the lower end--which largely explains higher achievement scores. Most public schools, on the other hand, serve a much broader, more diverse group, including many students from the lower half of the curve; thus, their achievement scores are lower. Many large inner city schools primarily are serving students at the lower end of the curve, or at least a much more diverse, broader segment of the population than are educated in most private schools.

Some public school systems from relatively well-to-do communities also primarily serve "advantaged" youths, and thus also show achievement scores which are superior to those from inner-city schools. Although richer schools are required to serve every child in their districts, the inability of disadvantaged youths' families to afford to live in more expensive housing eliminates many of these students from the well-to-do districts.

Through the years many claims have been made that private and more well-to-do public school systems provide better teaching than those in inner city areas; higher achievement test scores have often been provided as proof of this. Furthermore, in recent years many publicly-elected officials have proposed that teachers in higher achieving schools should receive rewards on the assumption that "superior teaching" explains superior achievement test performance. Of course, most awards under such a policy would go to schools who serve students from higher income, better-educated families--students primarily from the upper half of the curve. The frequency of such awards to inner city schools would be much lower.

Does higher achievement in the private and richer public schools mean their teachers are better than those in inner-city schools? Perhaps. But a large part of the difference in achievement probably is explained by the fact that the schools to a large extent are serving different populations with differing potentials for learning. Simply stated, the playing fields are not level.

If increased academic gains of students at private and richer schools were accounted for primarily by superior teaching, this could be easily demonstrated by teacher exchange programs for groups of inner city vs. well-to-do public and private school teachers. If the latter are indeed superior, then their inner city students' achievement should increase considerably beyond usual gains in a school year. Inner city teachers would be glad to learn how to teach more effectively.

Anyone claiming that some schools are superior to others due to achievement test results should be required to back such statements with data which make comparisons only after achievement test results have been statistically adjusted for differences in parental income, education, occupational levels, and IQ's of students, if available. Local universities are full of educational and psychological researchers who could perform this procedure for a nominal fee.

Also, any government-subsidized program which purports to award monies for superior teaching based on achievement test results should also be required to statistically adjust test results for differences in income, education, occupational levels, and IQ's. While such statistical manipulations will probably fail to eliminate all differences which exist between the achievements of the different populations being served, they will certainly provide a major step in that direction.

ACHIEVEMENT TESTING

Despite widespread use of testing in the schools, many people have very little understanding how to interpret achievement test results. Much of the confusion is due to lack of awareness of the different results which come from different types of achievement tests.

The three types of tests most frequently used to assess achievement in our schools follow:

- Criterion-Referenced Tests--Sometimes called mastery or competency-based tests, results from these tests show how well students have mastered different subject areas, such as reading. Test items are often ordered or divided by grade levels. Results are often presented as "grade level" scores, or number of correct responses, and show the degree to which the student has mastered the graded materials.

  Results are based on each student's performance in relation to the graded materials. No comparison is made to other students' performances.

  One type of criterion-referenced test that has grown in popularity in recent years is minimum competency tests, which utilize minimum cutoff scores for students to be promoted from grade to grade or to graduate from high school.

• Standardized Tests--Sometimes called norm-referenced tests, results from these tests show how well students perform in comparison to students of similar age or grade in the norm group. The norm group is the group of students used during test development to establish tables of expected scores for students of different ages or grades.

Standardized tests do not usually give information regarding what grade level the student is on.

Test items are not divided by grade level; instead, a variety of items are presented which begin at a very low level and go up to a very high level.

Raw numbers of correct responses from the students used to norm the test are compiled into distributions by students' ages or grades. These achievement scores usually form a normal or bell-shaped curve. (see Individual Differences)

Percentiles are assigned which show how a student compares with others of similar age or grade. When later administered to children in the schools, a student who gets a 30th percentile score in math is doing better than 30 per cent and less well than 70 per cent of the students of his age or grade used to establish the norms of the test.

Students who earn raw scores equivalent to the average for their grade should be assigned a percentile close to 50 and a "grade equivalent" score very close to actual grade placement. For example, a beginning seventh grader who scores average for his group might be assigned a grade equivalent score of 7.1, which indicates about one month into the seventh grade.

Grade equivalent scores are calibrated for all other possible raw score results according to how far they fall above and below the average on the normal curve for each grade.

Unlike grade level scores, grade equivalent scores are based on how each student's performance compares with that of the group of students used to develop the norms for the test-- not on the grade level of material mastered.

Stanine scores (which stands for "standard nine") are sometimes used, in which test results are assigned values from 1, which is very low, to 9, which is very high; a result of 5 is about average. Other standard scores are also reported, but whether stanines, other standard scores, grade equivalents, or percentiles are used, they all show how one child's performance compares with results of students of similar age or grade in the norm group. None has much to say about grade level functioning. In fact, comparisons of grade equivalents with grade level scores on other tests are often quite different.

- Open-Ended or Essay Tests--Results from these tests show the extent to which students meet subjective criteria, such as understanding of material and organization of thoughts. Students are usually required to respond in writing to one or more questions, and judges score the results based on pre-determined criteria. Scoring is quite subjective in that, even when using similar criteria, different judges scoring the same tests often assign quite different scores.

Unfortunately, many parents, elected officials, journalists, and even some professional educators make mistakes when interpreting achievement test results. The mistakes they make are largely due to failure to understand the different kinds of results which come from different types of achievement tests.

Unfortunately, even some superintendents of schools are lacking in basic knowledge about standardized achievement tests which are given in their schools. A few years ago a superintendent of a very large metropolitan school system bragged publicly that about sixty seven per cent of his students were "above grade level," thus confusing grade equivalent with grade level scores. Instead of showing his students were above grade level, test results actually showed many of his students were performing higher than those in the norm group. The test developers were so alarmed to hear that results were so skewed from this large school system that they renormed the test. Subsequent test (grade equivalents) results showed about half the students were above, and half were below, their actual grade placement.

Did academic performance levels plunge from one test administration to the next? Probably not. What really changed was the competency of the norm group the students were being compared against.

Sometimes parents also confuse grade equivalents from standardized tests with grade level scores from criterion-referenced tests. When this happens, the parent whose seventh-grade child has a 6.0 grade equivalent score in reading might wrongly conclude the child is reading one year below grade level, while it actually indicates the child is performing like the average student at the 6.0 grade in the norm group. The student could actually be on grade level in reading at his particular school, even though his grade equivalent was only 6.1.

A parent recently asked if her seventh grade daughter who earned a 12.1 grade equivalent score in math could enroll in a senior high math class, like trigonometry or calculus. The answer, of course, was "no." There's a big difference between performing in math like the average of beginning high school seniors (many of whom did not take advanced math courses), and demonstrating competency in advanced, twelfth grade math concepts, such as calculus.

Entire communities have become very excited when substantial percentages of students earn grade equivalent scores below their current grade placement. While everyone assumes this trend means students are below grade level, it really shows the students aren't performing as well as the norm group.

Could such results be attributed to inferior teaching? Perhaps, particularly if results show a downward trend on the same standardized test over a number of years with no major change in the school population. But they could also be attributed to the selection of a standardized test with a norm group that is not representative of the community in question.

In similar fashion, communities which have large numbers of students performing above their grade placement might incorrectly assume students are functioning above grade level, perhaps as a result of superb teaching or superior leadership in the schools. Once again, such conclusions might not be true.

The bottom line here is that grade equivalent scores from standardized tests should not be confused with grade level scores. If grade level results are desired, criterion referenced tests should be given which reflect curricular objectives within the school system. Or better yet, if parents really wish to know information about grade level functioning, why not simply rely on teacher reports? Every competent teacher should be able to provide information about how each child is functioning in all subject areas. This practice would not only save millions of achievement testing dollars--which could be used to hire more reading teachers--it would also eliminate much confusion surrounding testing in the schools.

The recommendation is made that all professional educators and any journalist or public official who either report on test results, or make policy which influences public schools, should take at least one course in introduction to educational or psychological tests and measurements. They owe it to the populations they serve to have a good understanding about the tests and results on which their reporting and policy making are based.

Finally, schools which have testing programs should provide free workshops to parents and others who wish to know more about the tests which are given to children and how to interpret results.

We should all be wary of self-contained instructional packages or computerized programs which come with criterion-referenced competency tests. Such programs often begin with a pretest to establish performance baselines and end with post-testing. All too often, promotions of such programs make exorbitant claims (at exorbitant prices) involving rapid growth of academic skills.

Several reading programs of this type have been sold with claims that students make gains up to four grade levels from pre- to post-testing. Unfortunately, some of these programs simply teach students to do well on the test, and leave major gaps in generalized abilities.

Results would be more impressive and more believable if similar gains would be demonstrated using reading tests which are not part of the instructional program and which are administered by independent parties who have no stake in the outcome.

Ideally, these tests could be used in pre- and post-testing both for classes on the special reading program and others on traditional reading programs. Consistently greater gains for the special reading groups over traditional groups would be much more impressive than self-contained programs which merely teach to the test. For that matter, such objective evidence should be demanded for the effectiveness of any new expensive instructional program which purportedly results in greater academic gains.

A few additional comments need to be said about high school graduation testing requirements. We support a pass/fail skills test to demonstrate competency in basic academic areas. However, such a program will have value only if no exceptions are made--for special education students, hardship cases, exceptional athletes, or any others who fail to pass the test.

The reason for no exceptions is that the testing program will have no value unless it is equitably applied throughout the schools--unless it really means that every student who passes has met minimum basic academic skills requirements. Otherwise, results would be worse than meaningless--they would be misleading.

Perhaps changes through our courts could be made which would permit dual-level diplomas. Under such a plan, all high school students would be required to meet curricular requirements for graduation. However, those who earn a passing score on the graduation competency test would get a Level I diploma, while those who fall short of a passing score would get a Level II designation. In this way, all students who meet curricular requirements could graduate; but colleges, future employers, and others could benefit from this additional information about basic skill levels.

EPILOGUE

The authors are sorry if some parts of this book offend or upset some people. Our intent is to stimulate dialogue which is needed to improve our nation's schools. Nevertheless, upsetting some people is a small price to pay for saving our children.

ABOUT THE AUTHORS

Stella Crawford holds licenses in elementary education, learning disabilities, mental retardation, emotionally disturbed, school administration, counseling, marriage and family therapy, and social work. Ms. Crawford has more than twenty years experience working in various public schools--and nearly as much experience attending them. She has taught elementary, middle, and high school students. She has been a school counselor, dean, department head, special education consultant, administrator, and social worker. She is also an adjunct university faculty member who teaches courses in psychology, and has a private marriage and family therapy practice. Ms. Crawford is also an experienced waitress, retail clothing salesperson, pizza maker, grill cook, library assistant, Girl Scout leader, camp art counselor, and insurance file clerk.

Phillip Vandivier has masters and doctoral degrees in school psychology, has a lifetime license to practice psychology in the public schools, is a licensed psychologist, and is a Certified Health Service Provider in Psychology. He worked nearly ten years in small town, large metropolitan, and suburban school districts as a school psychologist, private psychological consultant, and director of special services. Dr. Vandivier has extensive experience performing applied behavioral science research, has a private practice in psychology, and teaches university classes in general psychology, developmental psychology, educational psychology, and abnormal psychology. He also has worked as a hot dog vender, swimming pool attendant, file clerk, clerk typist, printer, warehouse worker, and assistant to a janitor.

The authors have published numerous journal articles and developed the *Written Expression Test,* which assesses written expression ability and the *Functional Word Kit,* which teaches survival reading skills.

They enjoy planting trees and feeding ducks, other birds, and rabbits in their small back yard.

None of us can be accurately summarized by what we have done to earn a living. All of our life experiences come together to make us the people we are. We hope the sum of our experiences have come together in a meaningful way that will enhance the lives of tomorrow's children.

To order additional copies of **Our Schools: What Happened? How To Fix Them**, complete the information below.

Ship to: (please print)

Name_____

Address_____

City, State, Zip _____

Day phone_____

_____ copies of *Our Schools: What Happened? How To Fix Them*

@ $26.50 each $ _____

Postage and handling @ $2.75 per book $ _____

IN residents add 5% tax $ _____

Total amount enclosed $ _____

Make checks payable to Psychological/Educational Publications

**Send to: Psychological/Educational Publications
P.O. Box 50626 • Indianapolis, IN 46250**

To order additional copies of **Our Schools: What Happened? How To Fix Them**, complete the information below.

Ship to: (please print)

Name_____

Address_____

City, State, Zip _____

Day phone_____

_____ copies of *Our Schools: What Happened? How To Fix Them*

@ $26.50 each $ _____

Postage and handling @ $2.75 per book $ _____

IN residents add 5% tax $ _____

Total amount enclosed $ _____

Make checks payable to Psychological/Educational Publications

**Send to: Psychological/Educational Publications
P.O. Box 50626 • Indianapolis, IN 46250**